"In selling different is good. You need to stand out from the crowd of sales people and businesses that are trying to capture your potential clients' attention and money. In *OUTRAGEOUS Advertising, That's OUTRAGEOUSLY Successful*, Bill Glazer does just that. In fact, in reading it, **I discovered some great strategies to apply to my own marketing efforts**. Thanks Bill!"

Tom Hopkins
Author of *How to Master the Art of Selling*

"I learned long ago that there are ads that win awards and there are ads that make money. Bill Glazer's book is full of the latter. In fact, **I've paid copywriters $10,000 or more to write ads that weren't half as good as the ones in this book.** Grab your copy because you'll pay for it twenty times with your very first campaign."

Bill Harrison, Partner,
FreePublicity.com

"What I love about Bill Glazer is that he not only delivers OUTRAGEOUSLY Successful Advertising through traditional offline media, **he has conquered it <u>online </u>as well.** There isn't a business owner or entrepreneur alive who couldn't profit from this.

Derek Gehl, Co-Founder and Chief Creative Officer
The Internet Marketing Center
Internetmarketing.com

"I'm disappointed with and dislike this book. I am disappointed Bill has packed it so full and given away so much for such a small, token price and I unsuccessfully argued for stripping it back when I reviewed the manuscript. As-is, this should be a $1,000.00 or $2,000.00 info-product sold as a kit of resources, not a book sold for the price of a Starbucks® coffee and scone. As an author, I admit to some unhappiness at having the bar raised. He has made the job tougher for the rest of us by so badly over-doing it here. Your gain, our headache."

Dan Kennedy
Author, Speaker, Consultant
Dankennedy.com

"I read LOTS of business and marketing books... and a lot of them are really good. But "Outrageous Advertising" is one of the rare breed with specific, actionable techniques that I can start using IMMEDIATELY. In fact, you don't even need to read the whole book - I'm not sure Bill will be happy with me saying this, but you can open it to nearly any page and pull out one of the promotions and drop it directly into your business. Best of all, even though most of the examples are OFFLINE... the same techniques are going to work just as well in my ONLINE business."

Jeff Walker,
ProductLaunchFormula.com

"This is one of the best books on advertising ever written, full of simple, proven, practical techniques to get more customers immediately."

Brian Tracy
Author, The Way to Wealth

- CD of an **EXCLUSIVE GOLD AUDIO INTERVIEW:**

  These are EXCLUSIVE interviews with <u>successful users of direct response advertising, leading experts and entrepreneurs in direct marketing, and famous business authors and speakers</u>. Use them to turn commuting hours into "POWER Thinking" hours.

* The New Member No B.S.® Income Explosion Guide & CD (Value = $29.97)

This resource is <u>especially designed for NEW MEMBERS</u> to show them HOW they can join the thousands of Established Members **creating exciting sales and PROFIT growth** in their Business, Practices, or Sales Careers & Greater SUCCESS in their Business lives.

Income Explosion FAST START Tele-Seminar with Dan Kennedy, Bill Glazer, and Lee Milteer (Value = $97.00)

Attend from the privacy and comfort of your home or office…hear a DYNAMIC discussion <u>of Key Advertising, Marketing, Promotion, Entrepreneurial & Phenomenon strategies</u>, PLUS answers to the most Frequently Asked Questions about these Strategies

* You'll also get these Exclusive "Members Only" Perks:

- **Special FREE Gold Member CALL-IN TIMES:** Several times a year, Dan & I schedule Gold-Member ONLY Call-In times
- **Gold Member RESTRICTED ACCESS WEBSITE**: Past issues of the *No B.S.® Marketing Letter*, articles, special news, etc.
- **Continually Updated MILLION DOLLAR RESOURCE DIRECTORY** with Contacts and Resources Dan & his clients use.

To activate your MOST INCREDIBLE FREE GIFT EVER you only pay a one-time charge of $4.95 (or $8.95 for Int'l subscribers) to cover postage (this is for everything). **After your 1-Month FREE test-drive, you will automatically continue at the <u>lowest</u> Gold Member price of $59.97 per month. Should you decide to cancel your membership, you can do so at any time by calling Glazer-Kennedy Insider's Circle™ at 410-825-8600 or faxing a cancellation note to 410-825-3301 (Monday through Friday 9am – 5pm). Remember, your credit card will NOT be charged the low monthly membership fee until the beginning of the next month, which means you will receive 1 full issue to read, test, and** profit from all of the powerful techniques and strategies you get from being an Insider's Circle Gold Member. **And of course, it's impossible for you to lose, because if you don't absolutely LOVE everything you get, you can simply cancel your membership before next month and never get billed a single penny for membership.**

EMAIL REQUIRED IN ORDER TO NOTIFY YOU ABOUT THE GLAZER-KENNEDY UNIVERSITY WEBINARS AND FAST START TELESEMINAR

Name _____ Business Name _____

Address _____

City _____ State _____ Postal Code _____ Country _____

e-mail* _____

Phone _____ Fax_____

Credit Card Instructions to Cover $4.95 ($8.95 Int'l) for Shipping & Handling:

____Visa ____MasterCard ____American Express ____Discover

Credit Card Number _____ Exp. Date _____

Signature _____ Date _____

FAX BACK TO 410-825-3301
Or mail to: 401 Jefferson Ave, Towson, MD 21286

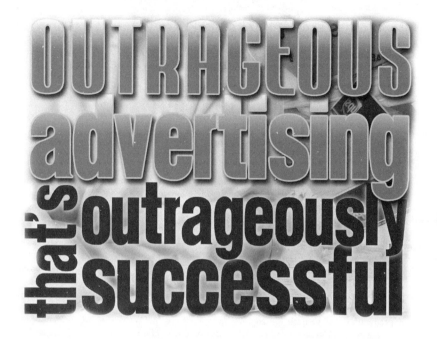

BILL GLAZER

foreword by Dan Kennedy

Glazer-Kennedy
publishing

an imprint of Morgan James Publishing
NEW YORK

BILL GLAZER

ISBN 978-0-98237-930-1 (paperback)

Published by:

Glazer-Kennedy publishing

an imprint of

Morgan James Publishing
1225 Franklin Ave. Ste 325
Garden City, NY 11530-1693
Toll Free 800-485-4943
www.MorganJamesPublishing.com

Cover Design by:
Megan Johnson
Johnson2Design
www.Johnson2Design.com
megan@Johnson2Design.com

Interior Design by:
Bonnie Bushman
bbushman@bresnan.net

Acknowledgments

I want to thank all of those who helped me become the person who could write this book. These are the special people who helped to shape my "OUTRAGEOUS Millionaire Marketing Mind." The list of people I could thank would fill up another entire book, but let me mention a few who had the greatest influence on me. There is my father, Harry Glazer, who taught me my prolific work ethic. Dan Kennedy, my mentor, who first showed me the "real" magic of marketing and continues to do so today. My management mentor, Vince Zirpoli, who taught me how to get so much done through others. My friend Brian Tarcy, who helped me to organize the book and kept me on the right path. The two very special ladies in my life, Karen, my wife, and Ruth, my mother, who always make sure I take the high road and do things the right way. Finally, I want to share my sincere appreciation for the dedication, hard work, and creativity of my second family, at the Glazer-Kennedy Insider's Circle offices.

Foreword
confessions from an ad man
by dan s. kennedy

I grew up in advertising and have spent thirty years as an ad man, at least in part. And I have an insider's confession. Most advertising is abject failure. It makes a lot more money for the ad agencies, production houses, and media than for the actual advertisers. At the corporate level, millions are spent on advertising that everybody notices but nobody remembers what it's selling, that wins awards but loses market share, and that is deliberately designed to defy accurate measurement and accountability. At the small business and entrepreneurial level, bland, vanilla, me-too ads are copied ad infinitum, in a parade of the blind leading the blind, again absent accurate measurement and accountability. As a result, just about every business owner goes through life endlessly disappointed and frustrated with his or her advertising, grudgingly investing, often only under duress or with an attitude of surrender.

Bill Glazer first changed all that in his own main-street retail businesses, then for several thousand retailers throughout America in his same category, and then for thousands more retailers in a wide variety of product categories, and now for an even broader range of businesses. I can't imagine there is another person who has as much influence and impact on business owners' movement from antiquated, traditional, poorly performing advertising to entirely new and radically different, direct-response-based advertising that consistently delivers extraordinary return on investment and competitive advantage. He is quietly cursed in some traditional advertising circles. He is celebrated daily by tens of thousands of business owners.

I have worked with highly successful business owners—from small, local shop owners to CEOs of privately held mid-sized companies including those on the Inc. 500 fastest-growth companies list to CEOs of companies as large as $1 billion in annual sales—and evaluated their advertising and marketing, for which I am paid very substantial fees, beginning at $16,800 a day. When I saw what Bill Glazer had done with his "advertising transformation" for his own retail businesses, I instantly recognized he'd braved the bold and outrageous to do something unique that could go far beyond simply turbo-charging his own stores' sales and profits. His results spoke loudly as well. I urged him to take what he had learned, developed, and perfected to the other business owners in his industry, and a new, influential change-agent was born; a literal revolution in advertising—in a rather stodgy retail category—was launched.

Thanks to this unusual book, you can harvest the best benefits of all this for your own business quickly and easily.

I say this is a very unusual book for three reasons.

First, its overall approach to advertising is not just different—it's *outrageously* **different!** Most books about advertising are anything but. They are, frankly, regurgitated mush with old labels papered over with new.

Second, it is based on *real-world, real-business results.* Maybe big company executives can afford the luxury of endlessly experimenting with ideas and theories about advertising birthed by fuzzy-headed professors at Harvard Business School and Madison Avenue's ad agency "creatives," who love drum-beating bunnies, talking and dancing lizards, and angry cavemen despite the fact that most consumers can't correctly name the products or companies being advertised, let alone enunciate any beneficial reasons to immediately seek out the product or company. Maybe they can afford such foolishness. You probably can't. But you CAN take confidence from the fact that every single one of the 108 different examples shown to you in this book, and by extension at its Web site, come from proven, successful use by real businesses. No matter how radical and outrageous it appears, it's the real advertising that really works. No other author on this subject has ever assembled so many completely proven, highly valuable examples in one low-priced book.

When I say "valuable," I mean it. On the rare occasions that Bill accepts private clients and develops advertising for them, he is paid such huge sums that most freelance ad copywriters are shocked and dismayed. To get any one of the winning campaigns you see here done for you from scratch could easily cost upwards from $10,000 to $25,000. This kind of experience-based expertise is pretty much unavailable to most main-street businesses—made accessible for the first time ever, right here. Further, these examples have produced, in aggregate, millions and millions of dollars for the business owners using them, and for many of the individual owners, transformed the competitive position and profitability of their businesses. Any way you wish to do the accounting, this book hands over to you more than a million dollars' worth of proven, profitable advertising easily translated and used by you. Further, there are breakthrough strategies for every media and purpose: yellow pages, newspaper, magazine, radio, TV, signage, direct-mail; attracting new customers or clients; bringing present customers back more often; upgrading customers; rescuing lost customers; bringing people in to your place of business in a steady stream or massive stampede; creating appointments for salespeople at your business or in the field—it's ALL here.

Third, it is a book to be used, *not* merely read. If you have a good, fun read and then place this on a high shelf, you miss the point and cheat yourself. It's actually a misnomer to even call this a book at all. It is more of a "magical toolbox," a cross between a sorcerer's secrets and a skilled mechanic's best tools, to be drawn from again and again, day in and day out; to repair your present advertising and fix the erratic and disappointing return on your present advertising investments; to build new and different ways of reaching out to new and present customers that amaze you with their results. This book provides the strategies you need to know and rely on; the samples that can speed your preparation of winning advertising and serve as essential shortcuts in a busy, multitasking business life; and the tools that belong right at your desk, at your right hand, to use to uncover and unleash your business's true attractant powers.

Incidentally, be sure to take advantage of the extensions of this book. The printed book you hold in your hands is actually one of several component parts of an entire advertising transformation system Bill has assembled for you. There is a *free* CD with all the samples and exhibits shown to you in this book, in full color and complete detail; a special Web site; *a free gift collection* of advertising, marketing, and business resources including a trial subscription to the *No B.S. Marketing Letter* and three Webinars; and referrals throughout the book to experts, specialists, and vendors who support implementation of all the outrageous advertising shown here.

Since I started with a confession, I'll end with one. I am disappointed with and dislike this book. I am disappointed Bill has packed it so full and given away so much for such a small, token price, and I unsuccessfully argued for stripping it back when I reviewed the manuscript. As is, this should be a $1,000 or $2,000 info-product sold as a kit of resources, not a book sold for the price of a Starbucks coffee and scone. I worry about it spoiling people. Or being taken for granted. Also, as an author, I admit to some unhappiness at having the bar raised. He has made the job tougher for the rest of us by so badly overdoing it here. Your gain, our headache.

PREFACE
who is bill glazer? why should you listen to me?

My name is Bill Glazer, and I have a crazy idea for you. How would you like to make OUTRAGEOUS amounts of money from your advertising?

You might be wondering right now why you should listen to a crazy idea from a guy in a straitjacket, and why, in fact, I am even in a straitjacket. The answer is simple: TO GET NOTICED.

You noticed, didn't you? Of course you did!

This is a book about OUTRAGEOUS advertising that is OUTRAGEOUSLY successful in a "must-see" kind of way. Here you will learn crazy-powerful tools to completely disarm the advertising-killing conditions known as clutter and boredom. In here, you will learn to create campaigns that shout: *Look here NOW!*

I cut through the clutter because I know how to get noticed, and I want to teach you how to use OUTRAGEOUS tactics to be OUTRAGEOUSLY successful too. It doesn't matter what you do. In fact, my OUTRAGEOUS strategies have been OUTRAGEOUSLY successful with entrepreneurs, service business operators, authors, speakers, consultants, e-commerce and Internet marketers, small business owners, B2B manufacturers, doctors, lawyers and others in private practices, sales professionals, and even people planning to start a new business.

On the following pages, you'll find that I've sold from inside of a jail cell (sorta!) and off the deck of a cruise ship steaming towards Alaska. I've gained customers by sending them a tiny garbage can in the mail and leaving a message from the King (aka Elvis) on their answering machines.

Of more importance, you'll discover that I am not shy, especially about making money, and I believe that customers only simply need to be reminded that they want to give me as much money as I desire.

So before we get started and to make sure we are right for each other, let me ask you a simple question.

Do you like money?

I assume that if you have a business and you're reading this book, you'd like more money. My goal is to lead you down the path where you don't make just more money; you actually make OUTRAGEOUS amounts of money. If this sounds good, then read on.

MY STORY: When I first joined my father's menswear business—Gage Menswear of Baltimore, Maryland—in 1974, I thought of marketing in the same traditional way that every other menswear business in the world did. We copied what every other menswear retailer did, treated our customers right, and hoped they would remember us the next time they needed to buy something.

At that time in Baltimore, there were fourteen menswear stores we were competing with. But over the years, the market changed and stores didn't survive.

There was movement from the city to the suburbs and changes in fashion, and our struggle in that market was to stay alive. No one actually believed we could thrive.

My father, in the late 1960s, had actually opened a side business to help troubled menswear stores either liquidate their assets or hold a big sale to get them back on their feet. I became part of that side consulting business when I joined the family retail business.

So, my early education was on two tracks: what I learned by working in the family menswear business and what I learned from consulting with other retailers.

You'll find it no surprise that the area I became particularly interested in, actually fascinated with, was marketing and advertising.

I began collecting customers' names, addresses, phone numbers, and purchase histories. I knew, based on their previous sales history, who to invite back and when to invite them. Of course computers, with point-of-sale software, helped a lot.

For instance, if a customer were strictly a sales customer, we would invite him back for a sale. If another customer wanted the "new" thing in the beginning of the season, we would invite him back when our newest merchandise arrived.

And all of this certainly helped us survive.

Meanwhile, I was reading a book a week, trying to learn about business and especially marketing. I was attending trade shows and going to the optional seminars—all with the goal of improving.

But it wasn't until 1995, when I was invited by a good friend to attend a success seminar in Philadelphia, that I really began to understand what it takes to market my business to its full potential.

There were a number of famous speakers there, including Zig Ziglar and Tom Hopkins. At the end of the seminar, there was a bonus speaker, a marketing guy named Dan Kennedy, whom I had never heard of before but perhaps became the most profitable happenchance meeting of my entire life.

As Dan walked towards the stage to speak, my friend suggested we leave, but I said I wanted to hear the marketing guy. It was the end of the day. At that point, about 9,500 of the 10,000 people in the hall had gotten up and left.

At first, I thought maybe I'd made a mistake by staying. I wondered if we should leave too. But we figured the parking lot would be jammed with everybody trying to exit at one time, so we stuck around to hear what he might say.

Within minutes, I was totally mesmerized. He said new and different things about marketing, things I had never heard of before. Best of all, it all made sense. It was astonishing, a true "aha" moment. I just kept thinking, "I should be doing this in my own business."

He had one idea after another, and they were all great—really great. So I ran to the back of the room to purchase his Home Study Tools and Resources and began to dive into them during the train ride back to Baltimore from Philly.

Then I did something that unfortunately few do. I put these tools and resources into motion in my business. He had actual templates that were smart and cost-effective. These were items that would have cost tens of thousands of dollars to produce myself.

I took his specific tools and reworked them for my business. This is what I call "S&D marketing," which you'll read more about in chapter 10. For the first time, I wasn't copying what everyone else in the menswear business was doing. I was creating my own marketing system using Dan's proven and successful concepts.

For example, I incorporated sequential mailings to a list of my customers that generated a response ten times better than I had ever experienced before.

My menswear business really took off.

Of the fourteen menswear stores that were in Baltimore in 1974, only one survived. My store, Gage Menswear, was the sole survivor. But more than that, we THRIVED.

How did we do it? I figured out how to get noticed and also how to be remembered with a systematic and yet OUTRAGEOUS approach to marketing that works.

Why does it work? I don't know. I am superman, but understanding why is not one of my superpowers. I really don't know why it works.

But here's the important thing to know: it doesn't matter why it works; it's ONLY important to know that it does work. In fact, it works OUTRAGEOUSLY well.

For example, one year I mailed a five-page handwritten letter on legal pad paper to 10,200 of my best customers telling them about an upcoming sale. You're probably thinking, "Who has time to read five pages?" I'll be showing it to you later in this book, but for now you just need to understand that this sales letter was the number-one most effective mailing I ever sent to my customers, and it has now worked equally as effective in dozens and dozens of businesses and industries.

In it, I told a personal story and I included handwritten SHAMELESS BRIBE coupons. I used different-sized writing and something about it seemed hopelessly amateurish, and yet it was all done by design because it also came across as compelling—something that demanded to be read.

Funny thing, this crazy mailing ended up winning the prestigious Multi-Media RAC Award at the 2002 Retail Advertising Conference.

2002 Multi-Media RAC Award

There were 500 entries, including many from major companies you have certainly heard of, but my little two-store chain won one of the highest awards given out in retail advertising. Simply OUTRAGEOUS!

But the best part wasn't the award. The best part was the results. Those were truly OUTRAGEOUS. And when you see the OUTRAGEOUS results that come from a well-developed OUTRAGEOUS campaign—taught in this book—you will realize that the only kind of crazy I really am is CRAZY SUCCESSFUL!

BACK TO DAN KENNEDY: Two years after I heard Dan speak in Philadelphia, I noticed he was coming to Baltimore to participate in the same seminar I heard him speak at before. I wrote him a letter, stating that I would love to take him out to dinner and thank him personally for what he had done for my business in the past two years (over a 53 percent increase in sales and profits).

So I was delighted when he responded and I had a chance to meet him personally. When we met, I used the time wisely and brought along a huge stack of direct-response advertising that I created over the past two years, including my first effort at OUTRAGEOUS advertising, which was a campaign that took advantage of a sprinkler malfunction I'd suffered in my store.

Gage Menswear Sprinkler Malfunction Ad

Dan was impressed. In fact, Dan was more than impressed. He actually suggested I go into business and teach other retailers how to use my strategies in their own businesses. And that's how this started.

Until that day, I had never considered that my strategies were something I could sell to others. It turns out—and I have lots of evidence—that my strategies are valuable to businesses in every field. And my most successful strategies are the OUTRAGEOUS ones because quite simply, OUTRAGEOUS advertising works.

Contents

1) Take The OUTRAGEOUS Path To OUTRAGEOUS Success

Dear Reader,

Since this is a book about <u>OUTRAGEOUS</u> advertising I felt compelled to start by writing you a letter to prove a point. You can always be ~~very~~ different and when you are, you get noticed.

You always get noticed!

Think about it. The only other time you've seen or even heard about a book that was mass-produced and handwritten, the production crew consisted of chanting monks. I'm no monk. I dress better with a different style haircut and a ~~much~~ much **bigger paycheck!**

My point is that by hand writing the beginning of this chapter, I forced you to notice and then be curious enough to ask, "I wonder ~~what~~ what this is about."

This is about taking the OUTRAGEOUS path and getting noticed.

1

OUTRAGEOUS doesn't always mean getting wild like me in a straitjacket. It can be as simple as changing the font in a letter you send off to prospective customers so that it looks like you wrote it **with your own hand**.

By the way, if you're wondering how to get your picture taken in a straitjacket, it's not as hard as you think. The first time I did it, I just rented one from a local costume store and had one of our staff take my picture with a digital camera. The one that you see on the cover was actually taken by a professional photographer in Dallas, Texas. (Douglas Bryan is a professional photographer who specializes in OUTRAGEOUS shots, including placing you in a straitjacket. He can be reached at (972) 642-2842 or through his Web site www.bryanphotography.com.

the path less traveled, think differently

The first mass-produced handwritten sales pitch I'd ever seen was a letter that was sent out by Dan Kennedy. He first saw this tactic used in a letter written by political candidate Ron Paul. As soon as I saw it, I knew that it was something different, and I've always looked for ways that others have used to cut through the clutter (see chapter 10).

It's not easy. The clutter of advertising messages can be overwhelming, but you must cut through it and understand that of the three possible answers—yes, maybe, or no—you have the best chance of getting a "yes" or "maybe" if you do something OUTRAGEOUS enough to get noticed. So I decided to try it at my retail store, Gage Menswear.

Handwrite a letter to my customers? OUTRAGEOUS!

But mine was more than just handwritten; it appeared spontaneous with big letters and small, wildly drawn parentheses, scratch-outs, and hand-drawn arrows pointing to a side note. And it was on yellow legal pad paper. Plus, get this—it was five pages!

C'mon! No one sends out a five-page handwritten sales letter. No one! I mean, who would read it?

Well, it turned out that lots of people read it. But more on the results later. First, take a look at the letter.

As you can see, there is a lot of copy in a five-page handwritten sales letter.
But here's the thing: it's not blah, blah copy; it all serves a purpose.
And if you study the letter, you will see there is even more.
I will summarize the approach.

OUTRAGEOUS yet systematic

This approach was not simply OUTRAGEOUS. There was madness, sure. But there was definitely a method to my madness.

I am about to give you an outline of the five pages. You can certainly see the progression and, in fact, the elements of OUTRAGEOUS advertising, which you will learn in detail in chapter 5.

OUTRAGEOUS resource

City Print specializes in printing on legal pads. To contact City Print, call 1-866-907-1222 or visit http://www.cityprintusa.com.

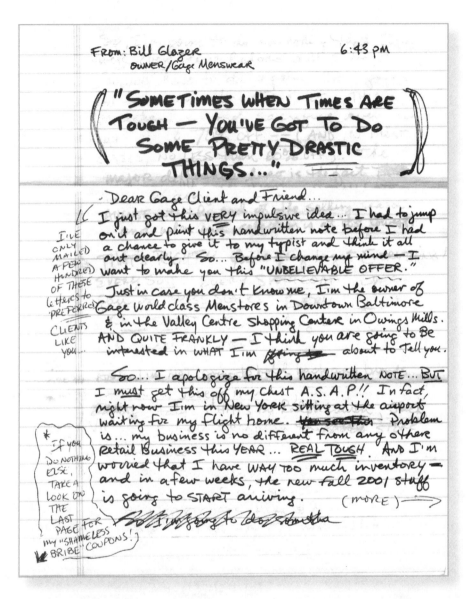

Page #1 of Bill Glazer's award-winning five-page handwritten sales letter
written on a yellow legal pad. You can see this in full color when you claim your
FREE CD of all of the exhibits in this book by using the form on page 312.

PAGE ONE - The first page, as you can see, introduces that a sale is going on, why I am writing the letter, and that the recipient of the letter is a preferred customer. I also note that the business is in a tough cycle and I need to do something drastic to reduce inventory before the new stuff arrives.

"Reason why" copy is critical for results. The response goes way up when you give the recipient a reason why you are making him or her an offer, and it is best relayed in the form of a story, as I did on page one of this letter.

That's right; everyone needs to know the reason you are doing something. What have we all heard about a free lunch? There's no such thing! No one believes in a deal that's too good to be true. So I gave the readers a reason why I was making what was about to be a tremendous offer and a reason why they were receiving a handwritten letter from me. (And in a side note on page one, I refer to "Shameless Bribe" coupons on page five of the letter.)

In fact, all great copywriters and marketers often use stories. People like hearing stories. It's because we were raised on stories. Our parents and relatives told us stories when we were children growing up, so we were trained to listen to stories.

So there you go. On that first page, I gave "reason why" copy in the form of a story.

OUTRAGEOUS exercise

Develop your business story.

- Why should people utilize your products or services?
- Develop a main story.
- Think of three others you can use for a particular offer or promotion or event.

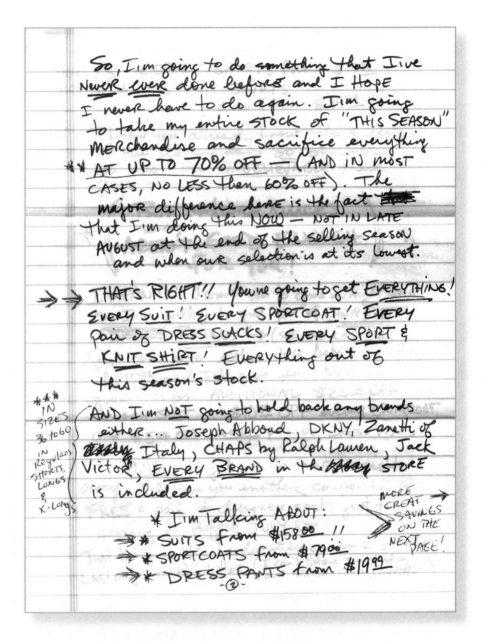

So, I'm going to do ~~something~~ that I've
Never **ever** done before and I Hope
I never have to do again. I'm going
to take my entire STOCK of "THIS SEASON"
MERchandise and sacrifice everything
** AT UP TO 70% OFF — (AND iN MOST
CASES, NO LESS then 60% OFF). The
major difference here is the fact ~~that~~
That I'm doing this NOW — NOT iN LATE
AUGUST at the end of the selling season
and when our selection is at its lowest.

⇒⇒ THAT'S RIGHT!! You're going to get EVERYTHING!
EVERY SUIT! EVERY SPORTCOAT! EVERY
pair of DRESS SLACKS! EVERY SPORT &
KNIT SHIRT! EVERYthing out of
this season's stock.

***
iN
SIZES
36 to 60

iN
Regulars
SHORTS,
LONGS
&
X-Longs

{ AND I'm NOT going to hold back any brands
either... Joseph Abboud, DKNY, Zanetti of
~~Italy~~ Italy, CHAPS by Ralph Lauren, Jack
Victor, EVERY BRAND in the ~~hairy~~ STORE
is included.

MORE ⇒
GREAT
SAVINGS
ON THE
NEXT PAGE!

* I'm Talking ABOUT:
⇒ * SUITS From $158⁰⁰ !!
⇒ * SPORTCOATS From $79⁰⁰
⇒ * DRESS PANTS From $19⁹⁹
-②-

Page #2 of Bill Glazer's award-winning five-page handwritten sales letter
written on a yellow legal pad. You can see this in full color when you claim your
FREE CD of all of the exhibits in this book by using the form on page 312.

PAGE TWO – The second page provides details of the offer—all the pertinent information. How much will I save? What's on sale? What brands? What categories?

Pertinent information is another key element when you are developing an advertisement. Just think about it. If you left out just one piece of pertinent information, it could make the difference (and often does) as to whether someone responds to you or not.

For example, let's say you are a dentist and you forget to list your phone number. How are potential or current patients going to call you to make an appointment?

Heck, I even know one company that forgot to put their name on their advertisement. I guess they're still waiting for someone to call.

OUTRAGEOUS exercise

List the pertinent information that prospects or customers would require in order to help them make a decision whether to respond to your advertising or not. Here's a partial list to consider:

- Name of the business
- Location
- Hours of operation
- Phone number
- Web site
- Items you sell
- Brands you sell

After you make your list, include it in its entirety every time you write your advertisements.

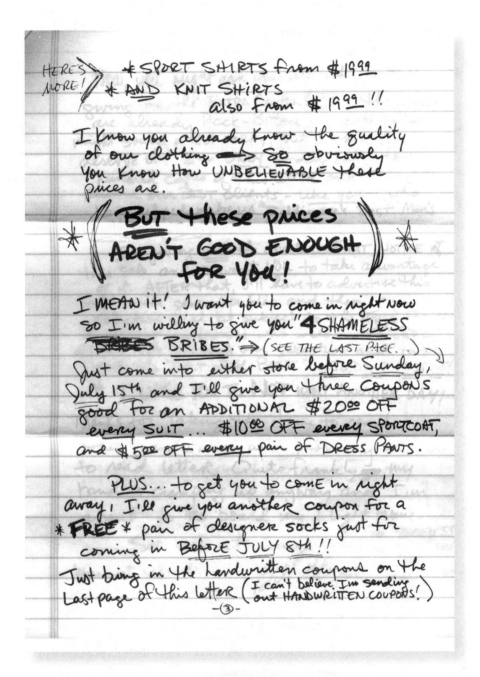

HERE'S MORE! → * SPORT SHIRTS from $19⁹⁹

* AND KNIT SHIRTS
                also from $19⁹⁹ !!

I know you already know the quality of our clothing → so obviously you know how UNBELIEVABLE these prices are.

* (**BUT these prices ARENT GOOD ENOUGH FOR YOU!**) *

I MEAN it! I want you to come in right now so I'm willing to give you "**4 SHAMELESS ~~BRIBES~~ BRIBES.**" → (SEE THE LAST PAGE...) ↘

Just come into either store before Sunday, July 15th and I'll give you three COUPONS good for an ADDITIONAL $20⁰⁰ OFF every SUIT... $10⁰⁰ OFF every SPORTCOAT, and $5⁰⁰ OFF every pair of DRESS PANTS.

PLUS... to get you to come in right away, I'll give you another coupon for a * **FREE** * pair of designer socks just for coming in BEFORE JULY 8TH !!

Just bring in the handwritten coupons on the last page of this letter (I can't believe I'm sending out HANDWRITTEN COUPONS!)

—③—

Page #3 of Bill Glazer's award-winning five-page handwritten sales letter written on a yellow legal pad. You can see this in full color when you claim your FREE CD of all of the exhibits in this book by using the form on page 312.

Once again, the handwriting itself, along with the copy, gives the letter tons of personality as well as personalized selling with hand-drawn arrows and asterisks and underlines and, well, writing. And of course, all of these wild, hand-drawn graphic messages are mixed beautifully with the specific message that you can save up to 70 percent on everything! And I name names of merchandise.

OUTRAGEOUS boost

Never make the mistake of thinking that current customers know everything about your business just because they've patronized you in the past. Include your pertinent information in every ad you create.

PAGE THREE – By the third page, the readers know why I am giving a sale, what is on sale, and for how much, but now I declare in huge bold handwritten print surrounded by big parentheses: (<u>BUT</u> THESE PRICES AREN'T GOOD ENOUGH FOR <u>YOU</u>!)

And I proceed to again mention the "Shameless Bribe" coupons first referred to on page one. This time, I give the specifics of what they are about and how much can be saved. One coupon is even for a free pair of designer socks just for coming into the store.

This free gift is called a premium, which can result in an increased response of as much as 30 percent. (For more, see chapter 8.)

Much of this whole approach is to let the reader of this letter know that I, Bill Glazer, am talking to him or her as a person and not some random number or customer. "I mean it," I wrote. "I want you to come in right now so I'm willing to give you '4 Shameless Bribes.'"

What you are trying to accomplish is for the reader to feel like you are writing specifically to him or her. Making the letter personal is incredibly effective, but this third page offers one more essential element: a deadline. "Just come into the store before Sunday, July 15 ..." You'll learn more about deadlines and why you must always have one in chapter 5.

Now, you might ask yourself, why is Bill giving me the EXTRA COUPONS?? ...the prices are already ROCK-BOTTOM... Well, this might sound a Bit CORNY, But I think You deserve it! I'm ONLY sending out a few hundred copies of this letter and I want to reward our BEST Clients – like you – who have helped make us "Baltimore's Best Men's Clothing STORE."

I'm giving you the absolute FIRST NOTICE of this sale and I want YOU to take advantage of it. AFTER that, J'll have to advertise this sale to the general public and then, my selection will be subject to the FREE-FOR-ALL of regular customers who will – NO DOUBT – Pick through our selection and take HOME the "BEST of the BEST" ...So, DON'T MISS OUT!

* **I URGE YOU TO NOT WAIT ANOTHER DAY!**

Thanks for Taking the time to read this handwritten and probably difficult to read letter. Quite frankly my hand is cramping up anyway and I'm about to board my flight home.

See you at Gage!

Warmest regards — Bill Glazer

(THE "SHAMELESS BRIBES" ARE ON THE NEXT PAGE) ⇒

-④-

Page #4 of Bill Glazer's award-winning five-page handwritten sales letter
written on a yellow legal pad. You can see this in full color when you claim your
FREE CD of all of the exhibits in this book by using the form on page 312.

PAGE FOUR – The fourth page is a personal message again reminding the readers that Gage is Baltimore's best men's clothing store and that they are my preferred customers; not everyone is getting this letter about these incredible savings.

I point the reader again to the "Shameless Bribe" coupons on the final page.

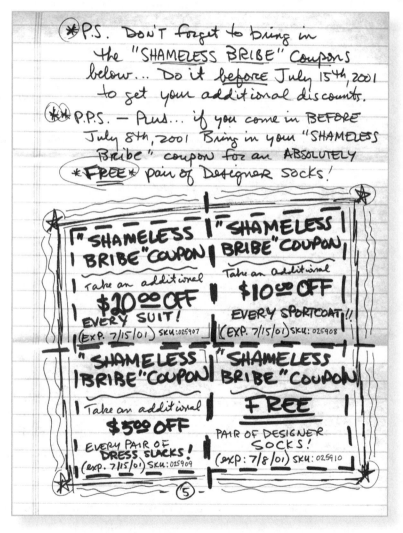

Page #5 of Bill Glazer's award-winning five-page handwritten sales letter
written on a yellow legal pad. You can see this in full color when you claim your
FREE CD of all of the exhibits in this book by using the form on page 312.

PAGE FIVE – This page includes information on the deadline as well as four hand-drawn coupons for savings on various types of merchandise— with deadlines.

The idea of a "Shameless Bribe" was funny and eye-catching, and it fit perfectly at the end of this long letter that appears to be written in a rush but is actually planned and executed.

OUTRAGEOUS exercise

Present your offers differently and people will take notice of them. So, develop three OUTRAGEOUS ways to present your offers as I did with my handwritten "Shameless Bribe" coupons.

1.

2.

3.

---

translating to other media

So now I had this wonderful letter that was generating results (more on that later) and I wanted to take advantage of what I had created out of an idea that I had swiped from a politician.

So I looked outside of the direct mail media for other ways to reach my customers with this obviously successful approach. And from my five-page sales letter I created a one-page newspaper advertisement that featured the "Shameless Bribe" coupons.

And then I also used this one-page creation as a fax that I sent out to the many customers who gave us their fax numbers. So this one OUTRAGEOUS creation translated into three media—all OUTRAGEOUSLY successful.

OUTRAGEOUS exercise

Review your previous advertising for ideas that were successful. How can you use these ideas in other media?

OUTRAGEOUS produces results from ... EVERYONE

As you saw in the preface, this five-page handwritten letter won the prestigious Multi-Media RAC Award at the 2002 Retail Advertising Conference.

But winning an award doesn't pay the bills. Money pays the bills, and this advertisement was my most successful ever. At my menswear stores, I had many successful campaigns. In fact, from 1996 to 2006 I delivered eighteen direct mail campaigns per year—each and every year. That totals 180 different campaigns. While most of them were successful, the five-page handwritten sales letter printed on yellow legal paper received the highest response of any of them.

Who responded? Presidents of banks responded. Board members of Fortune 1000 companies showed up for our sale. Accountants responded; doctors responded; lawyers responded; and they came to our sale because they saw a piece of mail in their mailbox that could not be ignored.

It looked handwritten. It looked important. So when the bank president/ doctor/lawyer came home from work, his wife gave him an envelope and said (we were later told), "You've got to see this. It looks important."

And it was important, OUTRAGEOUSLY important!

Now think about what I just said to you. People who you would normally think would not respond to five pages of UGLY handwriting responded. These are what we would normally categorize as educated, professional, affluent people, and they responded to a handwritten sales letter.

Whenever I deliver a seminar and show many of my OUTRAGEOUS examples to the attendees, there's always one or two of them who come up to me after I finish speaking and say, "While what you showed us was great, my customers won't respond to that kind of advertising because they're too sophisticated for it."

No, they're not! If it's interesting, people respond. Just as all kinds of people responded to my handwritten sales letter, they'll respond to your OUTRAGEOUS advertising. Everyone responds to OUTRAGEOUS advertising.

That's why I wrote this book—99 percent of small business owners are dissatisfied with the results they get from their current advertising. But it doesn't have to be that way. I am here to help. Remember, EVERYONE responds to OUTRAGEOUS advertising.

ideas are in every industry

A theme you will see emphasized throughout this book is that my best ideas came from somewhere else, and I am not speaking of a vacuum. I do business in the world, and so I pay attention to everything I see around me—especially other advertising.

The idea for the five-page handwritten letter, as you know, came from my first seeing the technique used by Dan Kennedy, who saw it used by a political candidate. I was in the menswear retail business. Why would I be looking at what a political candidate was doing? Wouldn't I have been better off looking at what other menswear stores were doing? After all, they knew what they were doing, right?

NOT!!!

I looked outside my industry. I looked for something that had never been done inside my industry. I looked for an idea I could translate successfully into my industry.

OUTRAGEOUS boost

If something is working in an industry, it will typically translate to others. In fact, it will often work better in others since it is new to them.

And the truth is, that's what I am always doing.

And I am looking for others who are looking for ideas as well, so I have joined Marketing Mastermind groups in the past and I continue to do so. In fact, I now lead three of them with over 140 extremely successful entrepreneurs.

In 1999, I was in a Marketing Mastermind meeting that was being facilitated by Dan Kennedy and others from over eighteen different industries. I was the retail guy. There was also a guy from the mortgage industry who was sending out pre-recorded messages that appeared on people's answering machines.

OUTRAGEOUS resource

There are Glazer-Kennedy Insider's Circle chapter meetings and Mastermind Groups in most cities throughout North America, run by certified independent business advisors. You can see if there's one in your area at www.dankennedy.com.

This had never been done in the retail world before, so I wanted to try it. I essentially brought voice broadcast into the retail world, and it worked. It worked great. In fact, the very first time I tried it, it resulted in a 92 percent increase in response when I added it to a previous successful promotion. This was a breakthrough I made by looking outside of my industry.

ideas are everywhere

Once I started developing OUTRAGEOUS advertising, I was always looking for opportunities to use it. Mostly because it works. But partly because it's fun.

When my wife and I went on a vacation to the Middle East, we went on a camel ride in the desert. Of course I had a picture snapped of me on a camel that I could send out to my customers. In fact, I sent it to the customers of my menswear stores and also to the members of Glazer-Kennedy Insider's Circle.

It made for big laughs and big sales.

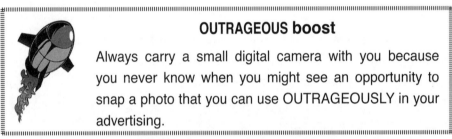

OUTRAGEOUS boost

Always carry a small digital camera with you because you never know when you might see an opportunity to snap a photo that you can use OUTRAGEOUSLY in your advertising.

I'm in the Negev Desert in the Middle East looking for you!! - Bill

You can see this photo in full color when you claim your FREE CD of all of the exhibits in this book by using the form on page 312.

In fact, I often view my vacations as marketing opportunities, and one of my best campaigns occurred when my wife and I went on a cruise to Alaska. Prior to the cruise, I had seen a postcard of the cruise ship with Alaska in the background. I liked it. I thought it would be a nice thing to send to my customers.

But I wanted to OUTRAGEOUSLY personalize it, so I wrote on the front of the postcard in pen, "Even when I'm on vacation, I'm thinking of you ..." and then atop the cruise ship, I drew a little stick figure with an arrow pointing to it that said, "ME."

You can see this in full color when you claim your FREE CD
of all of the exhibits in this book by using the form on page 312.

And on the back of the postcard, I put a coupon for $10 off any purchase, with a date to respond by.

And since I was actually heading on a cruise to Alaska, I wanted to mail the postcards so that they came with an Anchorage postmark. And I had a few customers.

I went to my printer and had them print up 10,146 postcards with this message that I wanted to send to my favorite 10,146 customers. Each was addressed, and I had stamps put on. All I needed was an Anchorage postmark. So I had my printer put all the postcards into a box and off I went with my wife on a nice vacation beginning in Anchorage.

When we arrived at the hotel, I went up to the clerk and asked if I could mail postcards at the hotel. She smiled and said sure. So I reached down and picked up my box of 10,146 postcards. I smiled back and told her that I wrote them all last night and my arm was killing me. We laughed. I continued on my vacation, and then when I came back home, I found out that the postcard campaign was a huge success.

As if you haven't already figured this out ... OUTRAGEOUS advertising not only works, but it is fun!

In fact, when I finally figured this whole thing out, it became the most enjoyable and fun thing that I did in my business.

OUTRAGEOUS exercise

Think of photo opportunities from everyday life or a vacation that can translate into an OUTRAGEOUS advertising campaign.

1.

2.

3.

defining results

The title of this book is *OUTRAGEOUS Advertising That's OUTRAGEOUSLY Successful*. I'd now like to take a moment to define what it means to be successful.

In this chapter, I showed you my five-page handwritten sales letter written on a yellow legal pad and I told you that of over 180 campaigns that I created for my menswear stores over a ten-year period, the handwritten letter received the highest response.

But achieving the highest response doesn't necessarily mean it was the most successful campaign I've ever created. In fact, as of the writing of this book, I've written nineteen sales letters that have generated more than $1 million in sales for my clients or one of my companies.

Certainly, the five-page handwritten sales letter was very ... very ... very successful for my menswear stores, but it didn't generate $1 million in sales for them.

So this brings me to how you need to define and measure what OUTRAGEOUSLY successful means. The way you define success is not by the percentage of response you receive. The way you define success is by the amount of money the advertisement generated versus the amount you spent to get it out.

This is what we call ROI (return on investment), and it is the only way I measure success—how much did you spend, and how much did you get back?

Sizzling Outrageous Summation

1) Always be on the lookout for OUTRAGEOUS opportunities to use in your advertising.

2) The more you tell, the more you sell. Don't be afraid of long copy to tell your entire story and pertinent information.

3)   Successful OUTRAGEOUS advertising can typically be moved from one media to the next.

4)   Everyone responds to OUTRAGEOUS advertising. Don't make the mistake of thinking your customers are too sophisticated for OUTRAGEOUS advertising.

5)   Study what's working outside your industry. OUTRAGEOUS advertising can often be moved from one industry to the next with terrific results.

6)   Join Mastermind groups to share ideas and network with other smart and open-minded entrepreneurs.

7)   OUTRAGEOUS advertising is fun, and it lets you make your business fun.

2) Defining Advertising And The Three Possible Responses

Most advertising stinks.

For instance, this has probably happened to you: some hotshot salesperson comes walking into your place of business and tells you that you've got to get your name out there.

Get your name out there? Um, what exactly does that mean?

"You know, get your name out there. Like Pepsi and Chevrolet or maybe Goodyear with their blimp."

It makes me want to scream, "Go away!"

See, here's the thing. If you're reading this book, you are most likely not like Pepsi or Chevrolet with unlimited resources to just get your name out there—and you probably don't have easy access to a blimp. That's not the way you run your business, or at least it shouldn't be. If the big esoteric task of brand building is your game, this is definitely not your book. Go away. I mean it.

On the other hand, if you are like the 99 percent of small business owners who are dissatisfied with the results they are currently getting from their advertising, then this IS the book for you.

The only type of advertising that you should be doing is what we call "direct-response advertising." This is advertising that is measurable and accountable. In other words, this is advertising that works.

So, if you are looking for advertising that produces real results, this is absolutely the book for you. I mean it.

My friend and business partner Dan Kennedy put it best: "The kind of advertising that you want to do is the kind where you pay for it with a check on Monday and it generates enough money so that you can cover the check by Thursday."

this is direct response, NOT BRANDING

Direct-response advertising asks the customer to respond and allows you to track that response. Brand building, on the other hand, is advertising that gets the name of your business, products, or services out there but you have no earthly idea whether or not it is paying for itself.

It's that simple.

Ninety-nine percent of all businesses cannot even think about brand building. Brand building will simply make you go broke. You may be told it will multiply your profits, but I contend that you can't multiply zeroes.

The kind of advertising I advocate does more than just get your name out there. It gets your message, your offer, and your deadline out there. Here it is; come and get it. Direct-response advertising does three specific things that I will discuss in detail in chapter 5:

- It makes an offer.
- It gives a deadline.
- It allows you to track response.

OUTRAGEOUS exercise

Go back one year and assemble all of the advertising you spent your hard-earned money on to promote your business and put them into three piles:

Pile #1: Brand-building advertising that promoted your company, but you have no idea whether it paid for itself or not.

Pile #2: Direct-response advertising that promoted your company, and you were able to track a good return on your investment.

Pile #3: Direct-response advertising that promoted your company and you know for a fact that you did NOT get a good return on your investment.

Now ... I want you to throw out all of your advertising that's in piles #1 and #3.

Finally, I want you to look at pile #2 after you finish reading this book and decide how you can take the lessons you've learned from *OUTRAGEOUS Advertising* and apply them to pile #2 to make the results even better ... OUTRAGEOUSLY better!!!

GOOD NEWS!!! often direct response leads to branding

If you do want to get your name out there, then I have some very good news for you. When you do direct-response advertising, and especially if you do OUTRAGEOUS direct-response advertising, you often get the by-product benefit of branding.

People start to know who you are while they are being urged to take direct action.

For instance, I sent out eighteen pieces of direct mail a year for my business at Gage Menswear. Because of this exposure, I knew that if I stopped advertising to my customers for a while they would still keep coming in the store.

Plus, I also knew from various national consumer surveys that my stores had the highest recognition factor of all of the competitors that were in my same category (menswear retailers).

You really do get the benefit of branding through direct-response advertising, but the best news is you don't have to directly pay for it.

yellow pages: a yellow brick road

A lot of people look at various media such as radio, newspapers, TV, and yellow pages and think that they cannot use this type of advertising as direct response.

That simply is not true. For example, let me show you how to use your local yellow pages as direct-response advertising.

Now before I show this to you, I want to make sure you understand that in most cases your local media salespeople hate it when you try to insist that you only run direct-response advertising.

Why do you think that is?

Well, the answer is simple. It's because they don't want you to be able to track results because they know that if you are able to accomplish that and do not get good results, you will likely stop advertising with them.

So, when you get a yearly visit from your local yellow pages sales representative, he or she will adamantly try to talk you out of running a direct-response ad and only place a brand-building ad.

How do I know this? Because if you pick up any yellow pages and look at the ads, just about all of them are brand-building ads, ads for which you can-NOT track results.

Try it yourself. Go to your local yellow pages and look at all of the ads in your particular category. What do you notice about them? Two things:

In very few cases can you track responses ... AND

They all look very similar, don't they?

Why do you think this is? It's because the yellow pages don't want you to know if you are actually getting a return on your investment. They don't even want you to have the ability to know.

Yet the great thing about the yellow pages (and every other type of media for that matter) is that you can still use it to do OUTRAGEOUS direct-response advertising.

On the next page is a great example of how to place a direct-response ad in the yellow pages. It was created by Larry Conn for his own carpet-cleaning business. In fact, Larry got so good at creating direct-response yellow pages advertising that he started a whole new business of teaching entrepreneurs in every field how to make this work for their own businesses.

Now let's take a look at Larry's yellow pages ad. First of all, it has a compelling headline (see chapter 5) and great testimonials (see chapter 7).

But those don't make it direct response, although they certainly make the ad more effective. What makes this direct response is the fact that there's a money-savings coupon in the ad complete with a dashed coupon border that allows Larry to track response.

The other thing that makes this a direct-response ad is the "Allergy Relief Hotline," which allows Larry to track how many people call it, and those people can also be transferred directly to Larry's office.

Larry can tell exactly who calls from this ad and how much they spend with him when they get their carpets cleaned.

OUTRAGEOUS boost

The "Allergy Relief Hotline" in Larry Conn's yellow pages ad is a great example of giving customers and prospects a secondary nonthreatening way to respond to your advertisement without them having to call a live person. Giving them a free recorded message to listen to will substantially increase response. See more about nonthreatening ways to respond later in this chapter.

OUTRAGEOUS resource

Larry Conn provides a FREE sixty-point evaluation of your current yellow pages ad. You can take advantage of this for your business at www.outrageous-advertising.com/yellowpages.

three piles of advertising

Most of your advertising won't find quite as targeted an audience as your yellow pages ad, but your goal will be to make it even more targeted. In order to do that, you must first understand a basic concept: people divide all advertising into three categories.

The easiest way to understand this is to visualize three piles of mail. I call these three piles "A" (the YES pile), "B" (the MAYBE pile), and "C" (the NO pile).

The A pile is what you absolutely have to look at this instant.

The B pile is advertising that you think you might be interested in but are just not sure about, and you set it aside for now.

The C pile is advertising that you absolutely have no interest in at all.

Fooled you with that B pile, didn't I?

We think we divide our advertising into only two piles—either YES or NO—but the truth is that much of the advertising we look at falls into the MAYBE pile as well. The MAYBE pile is often overlooked by most entrepreneurs, and it costs them a bunch of money. Not me. I don't overlook it. In fact, I teach it.

yes or no — or maybe later

The two top choices are clear and simple.

The A pile, which is the same as the YES pile, contains the things you must look at immediately. You feel compelled.

For instance, if you take a medical test and you are waiting for the results to be sent to you by mail, those results are part of the A pile. Yes, you want to open those immediately. Your child's report card falls into the same pile. This pile is not to be ignored because it is information you want and need.

The C pile, which is the NO pile, is exactly the opposite of the A pile. As soon as you see who it is from, you know you are not interested.

For instance, if you recently purchased gutters for your home, you are not going to be interested at all in an advertisement for gutters. Gutters? The answer is no—C pile.

However, life's choices are not always that simple.

Sometimes in business no doesn't mean no. It just may not mean yes. Instead, it may mean, "Let me think about it."

And though neither "no" nor "maybe later" is a successful sale, there is a huge difference between the two, and a successful business recognizes the opportunity of a "maybe later."

Of course, this means first recognizing the possibility of "maybe later" as an answer. And that's a challenge for many businesses that don't understand the basic psychology of a customer—EVERY customer.

options equal opportunities

Everyone is afraid of being sold.

And though the chances of a customer actually acting impulsively when something is interesting can be high, your first impression is not your only opportunity to reach a customer. Of course, that first impression is where OUTRAGEOUS has the most power, but there is a second part to it—the memorable part. Besides meaning "look here," OUTRAGEOUS means "remember."

And so simply understanding that the B pile—the "maybe later" pile—even exists is a start towards figuring out what to do with it.

Let's first look at two facts:

FACT #1:   *People want an alternative to "yes" or "no."* There are things that interest us but not enough to make an immediate decision.

FACT #2:   *People often want information without the pressure human interaction brings.* Sometimes it's just easier to read or listen to a recording at your own convenience. The "Allergy Relief Hotline" in Larry Conn's yellow pages ad is a great example of that; you can get more information without feeling threatened or being sold something by a live answer.

Understanding these two facts can set you on the path towards knowing how to deal with being in the B pile and getting the potential customers to take you from the B to the A pile.

So, we've seen two facts. Here is …

FACT #3:   *If you ignore them, they will ignore you.* You may be in the
            B pile, but you are not alone. Your potential customer is
            concerned with many things, and you are most likely not
            at the top of the list. Hey, it's not right. But it's life, and
            it's business.

People want to be reminded that they are important. Everyone wants
love. But as much as that, they want options—ways to respond and times to
respond. It's, of course, important to have deadlines (see chapter 5), but it's
just as important to let customers know that they can browse, shop, and buy
AT THEIR CONVENIENCE.

Information, especially in our modern connected times, is incredibly
easy to provide in an astonishing variety of formats, including:

- phone recordings
- Web pages
- Webinars
- tele-seminars
- free reports
- articles
- brochures

OUTRAGEOUS exercise

Look at the list below. Check off the ones you can use in your business to provide your prospects and customers with more nonthreatening information about your products and services:

____ Phone recordings

____ Web pages

____ Webinars

____ Tele-seminars

____ Free reports

____ Articles

____ Brochures

Now list all of the other places you can provide your prospects and customers with more nonthreatening information about your products and services:

_____

_____

_____

_____

_____

_____

Although your goal of OUTRAGEOUS advertising is to get immediately into the A pile, you must keep in mind the overall concept of what you are doing.

You are actually brand building by default when you land in the B pile. Either you are remembered or you are not. And the best way to be remembered, of course, is to offer something so good that the customer wants to directly respond. And so like all the great arguments, mine is circular, and my circle encloses your profits.

options equal profits

Once you figure out that you actually can move people from the "maybe later" B pile to the "yes" A pile, you can then discover amazing ways to leverage your position. By simply not ignoring this customer option, you are ahead of 90 percent of all businesses that think in terms of "yes" and "no."

Yet "maybe later" is a tricky category that requires due diligence. One of the best ways to move people into the A pile from the B pile is through sequential marketing, which we will talk a lot about in chapter 9.

And though that customer who put you into the B pile is a challenge, I look at this person as someone who actually wants to be a customer. How can you ignore someone like this?

My message is that you can't and you shouldn't ignore a "maybe later" customer because that customer is really a great prospect.

It's just a matter of paying attention until you are paid profits. Customers who think "maybe later" are thinking of reasons not to buy, and your job is to give them reasons to buy.

How do you give them such reasons?

Well, you give them options on how to find you, and then you remind them, over and over in OUTRAGEOUS ways, that you are their best option for whatever it is that you sell.

Sizzling Outrageous Summation

1) Branding is too expensive for 99 percent of all businesses.

2) Direct-response advertising must always have an offer and a deadline.

3) Direct-response advertising can lead to brand building, but you never want to buy brand-building advertising.

4) There are three possible responses to every ad: "yes," "no," or "maybe later."

5) When you pay attention to the "maybe later" customers, your profits will soar.

3) Applying OUTRAGEOUS Advertising

When I was first learning all these techniques that I am now teaching you, a disaster struck my menswear store. Well, it could have been a disaster. Instead, it was an OUTRAGEOUS success.

I came into the store one morning and discovered a sprinkler had malfunctioned and we had three inches of water in the store. I called the insurance company and made a quick settlement, and then I realized that most of my merchandise wasn't really damaged. Yet I had to liquidate it … F-A-S-T!!!

So I wrote an advertisement and put in all the facts.

Imagine that. I was so OUTRAGEOUS that I used facts!

The facts were these: I had a sprinkler malfunction; I made a quick settlement; and now I needed to sell merchandise … fast! I put the name of the insurance company and the policy number and other settlement information in the ad so that readers would understand this was real. (See the sprinkler malfunction advertorial in the preface of this book.)

I also presented the ad as an advertorial, meaning it was designed to look like an actual newspaper story. Thus, surrounded by real news, the ad looked like real news. So not only was I presenting the facts; I was presenting them as news. News you, the reader, needed to know.

I had a great sale, but here is the truly OUTRAGEOUS part. The insurance adjustor who handled my case saw my ad and wanted to know why I didn't put his name in there. So I ran another ad telling the story of my insurance guy, and the best part is, he paid for the ad!

Yes, that's OUTRAGEOUS.

OUTRAGEOUS exercise

How many occurrences can you think of that you can use in your marketing? List at least five occurrences that have happened in your business or life, like the sprinkler malfunction, that could give you a reason to contact your customers, patients, clients, or prospects.

Examples:

- Your marriage
- Your firstborn child
- Your child graduating from college
- A hurricane

Your Life Occurrences:

- _____
- _____
- _____
- _____
- _____

who cares why it works; it works!

Here's an interesting fact about the previous story and why I used an advertorial. I used an advertorial because they are read three times more often than other types of ads.

But why is that?

That's the beauty of this program. You don't need to know why. You only need to know that it works. These are not guesses I am presenting to you. These are proven OUTRAGEOUS techniques that work.

Why do they work? Who cares!!!

They work because people notice OUTRAGEOUS things. And what I am saying to you, and will repeat in detail in chapter 10, is that these ideas are the exact kind that you can use. I encourage you, as you will see, to swipe and deploy everything in here for use in your business.

Why do it? Because everything else is boring, and there is a lot of it out there. Each day, you may think you see twenty, thirty, maybe forty advertising and marketing messages, but the truth is that each person each day is exposed to about 3,700 marketing and sales messages. Thus, your job, as an advertiser, is to stand out among that clutter. Yes, each person sees 3,700 or so marketing and sales messages every single day. Most, we don't even notice because they are boring.

Cutting through that clutter and boredom is not easy—unless, of course, you are OUTRAGEOUS.

Daryn Ross as OUTRAGEOUS Superhero ... Megaman. You can see this exhibit in full color when you request the FREE OUTRAGEOUS CD-ROM by using the request form on page 312.

OUTRAGEOUS works everywhere

Can a superhero be OUTRAGEOUS?

Well, if you compare the superhero to everyone else in blue blazers and gray slacks, he sure can be.

Let me tell you about Daryn Ross, the owner of Megafast, a company that supplies promotional products. One of the themes of Megafast is that the company is fast. So when Daryn Ross was looking for a way to promote his business, he invented a superhero—Megaman.

When Daryn is invited, as he often is, to speak at a conference, he almost always steals the show. While others put the audience to sleep with mundane, ridiculous, and unimportant trivia, Megaman in a full superhero outfit (tights and all) takes the stage and suddenly commands attention.

His is not just a speech. It is a show as he quickly presents a one-minute video running at three times its normal speed (to show the company is, you know, mega-fast). Then the superhero, Megaman, pulls out a treasure chest, offering training videos and saying that the first 450 people to the booth by 2:25 today get a free DVD worth $297.

As you can imagine, his booth is packed with prospects because as I've proven to you ... OUTRAGEOUS works. The DVDs show his product line, testimonials, and how to enroll in a monthly telecoaching program. After they view all of that, they can print out bonuses, which are coupons for discounts off of products.

Megaman stands out in an industry of 3,000 or so suppliers because, as Daryn so eloquently states to me in a letter, "No other supplier in our industry would even dare pull a stunt like this ... they're all too professional."

OUTRAGEOUS exercise

How can you potray yourself as OUTRAGEOUS or use a character to promote yourself and your business just like Daryn Ross did with Megaman and I did when I jumped inside a straightjacket for the cover of this book?

Write down three different ways you can portray yourself or incorporate a character of some kind into your marketing.

Example: Take a picture of yourself behind a metal fence that looks like you're in a prison cell.

Then write down how you can use it in your marketing: Our Prices Are So Low ... You'll Swear It's Illegal

#1 OUTRAGEOUS character I can create: _____

_____

_____

How I can use it in my marketing: _____

_____

_____

#2 OUTRAGEOUS character I can create: _____

_____

_____

How I can use it in my marketing: _____

_____

_____

#3 OUTRAGEOUS character I can create: _____

_____

_____

How I can use it in my marketing: _____

_____

_____

OUTRAGEOUS boost

Daryn Ross won the coveted title of Glazer-Kennedy Insider's Circle Marketer of the Year at the 2007 MARKETING & MONEY-MAKING SuperConference. He's a great example of someone who has applied the OUTRAGEOUS principles taught in this book to turn his company into an industry leader.

Daryn is professionally OUTRAGEOUSLY successful. How's that for professional?

One thing that Daryn Ross proves is that this concept of OUTRAGEOUS works in many places in many ways. Newspaper advertisements or direct mail are just part of a bigger picture that includes, if you want, even superheroes.

help wanted OUTRAGEOUSLY

Bill and Steve Harrison of Philadelphia own Bradley Communications Corp. (www.FreePublicity.com), which helps authors market their books and entrepreneurs get free publicity on radio/TV shows and in major magazines. Since many people know that a book is the best calling card, granting instant credibility, the business is very successful and busy. Well, it was so busy that they needed an assistant.

OUTRAGEOUS resource

Bill and Steve Harrison publish *Book Marketing Update*, a monthly newsletter that tells authors about successful book promotion campaigns as well as publicity opportunities in major magazines, newspapers, and radio/TV shows. If you have a book that you would like to get exposure for, go to www.MillionDollarAuthorClub.com (or FreePublicity.com for their other resources).

FH2503

Office Help Wanted Now!

Could you be the great assistant I'm seeking to work part-time and handle many of the pesky administrative details of running my growing Lansdowne business?

Busy business owner constantly buried with far too much to do needs very organized, detail-oriented assistant 28 hours weekly in his Lansdowne office

It's 10:07 pm on a Wednesday night and I'm still in my office working!

My brother and I own a rapidly-growing publishing company located in Lansdowne, where we've been for 16 years now.

I'm stuck working late again tonight because I've just got too many things to do --- all the paperwork, invoices, schedules, faxes and adminstrative details that go with running a business are killing me!

Can you help make my headaches vanish by handling some of these details?

Are you somebody who's superb at handling details ... a loyal, hardworking behind-the-scenes type person who always follows-through and almost never misses a deadline ... so productive your last employer considered hiring two people to replace you after you left ... a strong typist with good computer skills ... comfortable in a small business environment where priorities can change quickly ... a super-organized get-it-done type person who's also very good on the phone talking with people?

If so, we should talk because you just might be the great assistant I'm looking for 28 hours a week (9:30 am till 3:00 pm, Monday through Fridays). The pay is negotiable and our office dress code is casual. I don't care if you haven't worked in a while and you don't need a resume to apply.

Think you might be the person I'm looking for? For more details, pick up the phone now and **call my 24-hour voice mail at 610-259-0707 x760**

Hopefully with your help I'll be able to start leaving work at a decent hour!

Bill and Steve Harrison's OUTRAGEOUS help-wanted newspaper flyer.
You can see this exhibit in full color when you request the FREE
OUTRAGEOUS CD-ROM by using the request form on page 312.

They had tried finding an assistant in the usual newspaper help-wanted-ad kind of way, but they couldn't find a successful candidate.

So they tried something OUTRAGEOUS. They wrote a one-page very personal help-wanted plea. "Could you be the great assistant I'm seeking …" it began.

This was inserted as a free standing insert (FSI) in a regional distribution of a Philadelphia newspaper, and it was so successful that 600 people applied for the job, including some who were perfectly qualified.

They found a great hire and proved again that OUTRAGEOUS advertising works anywhere.

OUTRAGEOUS in vegas

I've been six times to see Dr. Scott Lewis's Wild Comedy Hypnosis Show at the Riviera in Las Vegas. I love it. It's terrific.

So when Scott asked me to help him promote his show, the first thing I looked at was how he was already promoting his show. And he told me about rack cards—a kind of promotional material about local tourist attractions. You've certainly seen them. They are displayed in almost every hotel in America.

OUTRAGEOUS boost

There's an old saying in marketing that LITTLE HINGES CAN OPEN BIG DOORS. Look for little changes that you can make that will open up your big doors to greater response.

Well Scott, who is a retired chiropractor (thus, Dr. Scott), showed me his rack card, and the one thing I noticed immediately was that when the card was actually in the rack, you only saw the top two inches. It wasn't until you

OUTRAGEOUS exercise

Create your own OUTRAGEOUS help-wanted flyer.

Most businesses are looking for good employees from time to time but don't consider this creative alternative to the usual methods. In this exercise, create a narrative that describes your reason for needing help, the duties that will be performed, and the type of person you want. Start by making these lists.

These lists will help you write your ad.

Reasons for requiring new or replacement hires:

1.

2.

3.

4.

5.

Duties:

1.

2.

3.

4.

5.

Skills Required:

1:

2:

3:

4:

5:

Finally, list all of the newspapers in your area and all other places you can post it:

1.

2.

3.

pulled the card out of the rack that you could see the wild picture of Scott with images of his hypnotized subjects next to him.

So we simply changed the design of his card so that the top included the title "DR. SCOTT'S WILD COMEDY HYPNOSIS," the offer (which was cheap by Vegas standards, and thus a deal), and the words "Includes FREE SOUVENIR."

Dr. Scott Lewis's OUTRAGEOUS rack card. You can see this exhibit in full color when you request the FREE OUTRAGEOUS CD-ROM by using the request form on page 312.

This small yet OUTRAGEOUS change to the design of the card brought about OUTRAGEOUS results. Scott's results tripled from the change in design. Those are hypnotic OUTRAGEOUS results!

OUTRAGEOUS exercise

Look at all of your advertising and ask yourself, "What's the first thing that people see when they look at it?"

Look for ways to make changes to that first impression the same way that Dr. Scott Lewis made changes on his OUTRAGEOUS rack card that could generate a big increase in response.

selling the statler brothers OUTRAGEOUSLY

Publishing Group of America, which is selling CDs and DVDs of the Statler Brothers' Final Appreciation Farewell Concert, is a member of Glazer-Kennedy Insider's Circle, my marketing company that provides cutting-edge advice to entrepreneurs.

Publishing Group of America's OUTRAGEOUS Statler Brothers newspaper advertorial-style ad. You can see this exhibit in full color when you request the FREE OUTRAGEOUS CD-ROM by using the request form on page 312.

They had been running an ad advertising the concert for a year when they contacted me and took my copywriting course and signed up for my newsletters. And then they changed their advertisement to include many of the techniques I taught, including using headlines and even using highlighting as you did when you were in school.

Their results were phenomenal. But just to be sure, they tried running their old ad one more time. The comparison was this:

OUTRAGEOUS advertising improved results 53.2 percent!

It's enough to make you want to sing along.

an OUTRAGEOUS sign selling results not products

In Blackwood South, Australia, Julie Thorp manages Reflection Skin and Body Care, and she sells body wraps, among other things. These wraps are designed, in the course of three $130 treatments, to help a woman drop a dress size.

Julie Thorpe's OUTRAGEOUS
Window Sign
to sell body wraps: You can see
this exhibit in full color when you
request the FREE OUTRAGEOUS
CD-Rom by using the Request
Form on page 312

But she rarely advertised them, and if she did, she mentioned the product— body wraps.

After applying my OUTRAGEOUS information, she came up with a new idea for a sign that would sell not the wrap but the result. Her sign said, "drop a dress size!"

In her letter to me, she wrote, "Before this sign, we would be lucky if we did one of these treatments every month. Since I put this sign out we do a minimum of 40 on average a month. Plus they pay for a course of treatments and take home the prescribed products to go with the body wrap and they book in for other services we provide. As you can see, these are very good dollars!!"

You could even call them beautifully OUTRAGEOUS.

OUTRAGEOUS exercise

More than 30 percent of all buying decisions are made when people read signs—either inside or outside of a business.

Take a site survey of your business for places it makes sense to display a sign that a customer or prospect will see. Create a sign for that specific spot.

OUTRAGEOUS on the radio, #1

Vicky Irvin, who teaches a real estate investment seminar and then sells educational material, found that a string of bad news about real estate in general was beginning to affect her business.

She had been running radio advertisements for her seminar, but she found that free attendance at her seminar was running at half of its normal 500 people. So she took action.

She decided, in OUTRAGEOUS fashion, to attack the facts head-on. This is how her new, OUTRAGEOUS ad began.

> *My name is Vicky Irvin, the Real Estate Investment Queen. You've seen **the lies** on TV. You've seen **the lies** in the newspaper. They say it's a bad time to get involved in real estate.*
>
> ***They're all lies**.*

From there, she dropped in two testimonials from satisfied students and an offer to receive her free CD.

Response to this ad brought attendance back up to the pre-slump number of 500 per seminar.

OUTRAGEOUS on the radio, #2

I was asked by Levinson's Menswear of Petersburg, Virginia, to help with a liquidation sale.

In order to have the most successful sale possible, I recalled one basic rule of OUTRAGEOUS advertising: people notice celebrities.

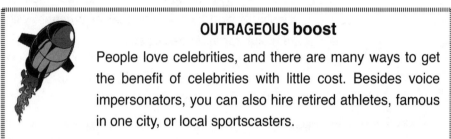

OUTRAGEOUS boost

People love celebrities, and there are many ways to get the benefit of celebrities with little cost. Besides voice impersonators, you can also hire retired athletes, famous in one city, or local sportscasters.

Okay, here's the best part, maybe even the most OUTRAGEOUS of all: you can benefit from celebrity recognition without actually paying a celebrity. For Levinson's, we benefited from Eddie Murphy by simply hiring an Eddie Murphy voice impersonator.

All you have to do up front is tell the listener, in the voice of the celebrity, that this is not the celebrity.

OUTRAGEOUS resource

The Great Voice Company offers professional voice impersonators at a reasonable cost. Their contact information can be found at www.getgreatvoices.com.

So here's the ad I wrote for Levinson's.

> *I'm not Eddie Murphy, man, but look I got something to tell you: Levinson's is going out of business FOREVER! No more, it's over, goodbye. They'll be going out with a last blast like you'll never forget. It's the going-out-of-business sale that's rockin' the whole*

> Petersburg area. Levinson's going-out-of-business sale and it's the last chance to stock up on the quality menswear Levinson's has always been famous for. Only now at 50 percent off! 50 percent! Not 25, not 30, but 50 percent off names like Givenchy, Pierre Cardin, J.J. Chochran, Adidas, and so many more. You'll see fine suits priced from just $57.50, great ski jackets from $42.50, velour warm-up suits from $47.50, stylish leather jackets from $112. 112 dollars! Dress shoes, shirts, slacks, designer jeans, dress coats, top coats, and all at half price! It's unbelievable! It's during Levinson's incredible going-out-of-business sale! Levinson's Menswear, at the corner of Washington and Sycamore. Just like the tree, it'll soon be a memory. So hurry in now for the best selection in Levinson's incredible going-out-of-business sale!

It's not Eddie Murphy. We say it up front. But the voice sounds just like the famous comedian, and the copy is funny. These two elements, taken together, offer an OUTRAGEOUS attention-getting advertisement that has to be listened to. And it was. In three weeks, the entire store was liquidated.

OUTRAGEOUS resource

You can hear this and other recordings mentioned in this book when you request the free OUTRAGEOUS CD-ROM.

automotive training institute mailing

So let's pretend you own an automobile repair shop in Minnesota and you receive an envelope addressed to you from another automotive dealer in the same area.

Why is he writing to you? You've got to open it, don't you?

Of course you do, and that's exactly what Chris "Chubby" Frederick, president of the Automotive Training Institute, located in Maryland, figures when he sells his training program. You're more likely to open a letter from another local automotive dealer than you are to open a letter from Maryland.

Minneapolis, MN ... you can attend from the comfort of your own office or hom *happening on January 30th, and if you are one of the first 47 repair shop own*

"Bill, what if there increase your car cou profit, attract and ke your stress in half ... smarter, not harder, i dreamec

- Chris *President of the Au............*

Chubby increased my car count & my cash profit. He can do the same for you. Look at this letter to see what he is giving away for

FREE... !

- Dan Robinson *Dan's Champion* *Mankato, MN*

January 24, 2007
Dear Bill,

Not too long ago, having a good auto repair shop with decent service was all it took to make plenty of money. No more. Today, dealers are blatantly stealing away your best clients with dirty tricks and cut-throat competition, quick-lube franchises are soaking up the lucrative maintenance business, margins are drying up, and car dealer vehicle retention marketing have car counts dropping like a rock.

Is it a hopeless situation or an amazing opportunity?

In the next 11 months a select few shop owners will make more money with less work and less stress than ever before. Their car counts will go up. Cash profit will increase to as much as 30%. Attracting and keeping motivated techs will become easier than ever before. Best of all, they'll be able to spend more time doing the things they love instead of stressing over the things they hate.

They'll do it all because of these 3 things:

1) **3 industry-shaking trends that hardly anyone is aware of and even fewer understand.** There are 3 trends picking up speed right now that will forever change the way the most profitable shops operate. They form a "perfect storm" that will destroy some shops (or leave them with bottom-barrel price shoppers as their only clients) and make a select few owners wealthy.

2) **Eliminating the "most wanted" list of profit-draining mistakes.** 99% of all shop owners make the same handful of profit-killing mistakes. These mistakes slash net profit, take the fun out of being in the auto repair business, and even result in unmotivated and disloyal techs. Most shop owners have no idea they are making these mistakes because the competition is doing the same thing ... and some industry "experts" even teach them as "best practices".

3) **Following a proven, step-by-step plan to greater profits.** Unfortunately, "theory" dominates the auto repair business management industry. What you really need to grow your business is street-smart advice about what really works in wildly successful shops in your area ... something I am uniquely qualified to give you. Let me explain...

My name is Chris Frederick, but everyone calls me Chubby. I've helped over 10,000 repair shops become more profitable over the last 34 years. My company, ATI, is the only management training team endorsed by the Tire Industry Association (TIA) and the Automotive Management Institute (AMI). I've written articles and been featured in Tire Review, Auto, Inc., and other industry publications. I'm not telling you this to brag. I just want you to know that I'm an industry vet who has seen it all ... good times and bad ... and I've never seen a better opportunity for smart owners to grow their businesses.

I feel so strongly about getting this information in your hands *while it's hot* that I'm doing something I've never done before: I'm offering you a limited opportunity to be one of only 47 Minneapolis-area shop owners on a FREE telephone seminar that will change your business forever. I'll reveal 3 trends rocking the industry and how to profit from them, profit-draining mistakes and what to do about them, and more. If you are half as serious about growing your business as I am about helping you do it, you can't afford to miss out.

Here are a few of the amazing secrets to repair shop success
I'm going to reveal on this FREE telephone seminar...

- **The raw truth about pricing best practices.** How to escape the "profit-killing loop" almost all shop owners get stuck in. Here's a hint: You cannot look to the competition when setting prices and establishing margins. I'll tell you why, how getting over this hurdle can add 30-50% to your net profit in less than 11 months, and what the only good source of pricing best practices is.

(please turn...)

Automotive Training Institute's OUTRAGEOUS letter.
You can see this exhibit in full color when you request the FREE
OUTRAGEOUS CD-ROM by using the request form on page 312.

- **What does it really take to attract high-quality, high-paying clients?** I'm not talking about someone who brings in a car, a case of oil, and an attitude about paying pennies for dollars worth of work. I am talking about clients who value quality and personal service ... clients who want you to care for their cars for a lifetime, including maintenance ... and clients who never fuss over price.
- **Escape the repair shop rat race forever.** Pay your bills on time, have money in the bank, and get more done by working fewer hours with much less stress.
- **"The marriage saver."** How a struggling, stressed-out and overworked shop owner and his stressed-out and overworked wife went from 18 hour days to taking several weeks of vacations per year. How much would being able to take days or weeks off "at-will" to spend with your spouse, children, or loved ones mean to them?
- **How a small "mindset shift" is the key to doubling or tripling the cash profits in your shop, and securing your own personal wealth and future.** Doing what you've always done, just harder, will never produce a quantum leap in your business. This "mindset shift" will, and I'll reveal it on the call.
- **Little-known "tricks" to hiring, compensating and leading techs so they stay loyal, motivated and help you to build your business** ... not just take home a paycheck. You'll even learn a simple "covert" test that will reveal what really motivates your techs. *It's rarely money, and I'll prove it to you.*
- **I'm even having 3 special guests on the telephone seminar.** These shop owners have put the strategies and tactics I'll be talking about to work and will tell you exactly how their businesses have transformed.

Claim your FREE spot before it's too late...

IMPORTANT: I'm sending this letter to over 4200 owners in your area, but I can only accept 47 attendees on this FREE telephone seminar. That means you can't afford to hesitate ... not even for a second ... or you risk losing your seat to a competitor who acts quicker. Do you really want them to have this information while you miss out?

The FREE telephone seminar happens twice on Tuesday, January 30th, first at 10AM and again at 7:30PM. You can attend the seminar that best fits your schedule. All you need is a telephone, a quiet spot to listen to the seminar, and something to take notes with. Register today by following the instructions at the bottom of this page.

Remember ... only 47 total seats available for this seminar. That's it. If you want to take part, register right now, while it's fresh on your mind and we still have space on the call.

C. L. Frederick

Chris "Chubby" Frederick, President of the Automotive Training Institute

- -

Bill, Your 3-Minute FREE Registration Form

"How Your Auto Repair Shop Can Quickly Add More High-Dollar Repair Orders & Attract More Cash Profit With Less Stress & Less Work Than Ever Before."

This FREE telephone seminar is happening on Tuesday, January 30th. There are 3 ways to reserve your spot right now:

1. Call **1-877-599-3879** and press **extension 7600** to register by phone. (Note: This is an automatic process, you can register even if it is 4 in the morning!)
2. Fill out this form and FAX it to 1-301-498-9088.

Shop Name: _____

What time is best for you to attend? (Circle one.)   10 AM or   7:30 PM

Your Name: _____

Mailing Address: _____

Your FAX Number: _____   Business Phone #: _____

(VERY IMPORTANT – your instructions to get on the telephone seminar will be FAXed to this number!)

Automotive Training Institute's registration form.

Chubby's OUTRAGEOUS approach to getting customers is to enlist existing customers to his cause. And so, as the owner of your own Minnesota automobile repair shop, you've now opened this letter, which came from Dan Robinson, owner of Dan's Champion of Mankato, Minnesota.

And by the looks of the letter, the first thing you see is a yellow Post-it note attached to what appears on first glance to be an ad from a newspaper. The Post-it note is from Dan, a local owner of an automobile repair business.

In handwriting on the Post-it note, Dan writes, "Chubby increased my car count and cash profit. He can do the same for you. Look at this letter to see what he is giving away for FREE…!"

And then there's the letter, full of all the elements you would expect in a proper direct-response advertisement—a headline, an offer, and a deadline. There is a picture of Chubby, plenty of descriptive copy about what is being offered, including parts highlighted in yellow as well as underlined.

It looks like a letter, and it looks like a magazine advertisement. There were many OUTRAGEOUS elements to this approach, and the results were equally OUTRAGEOUS!

OUTRAGEOUS exercise

Think of ways you can leverage your customers to help you, like the way in which Chubby got the letter advertising his service sent from one of his satisfied customers in a local area.

the bill glazer $100 business card

If I give you a business card, you want to keep it.

You want to show other people. You want to say, "Check this out."

My business card looks like money—fanned-out $100 bills. Yes, it's a keeper—as valuable as money. If you get my business card, you really do want to keep it.

Outside of Bill Glazer's
OUTRAGEOUS business card.

Inside of Bill Glazer's
OUTRAGEOUS business card.

You can see this exhibit in full color when you request the
FREE OUTRAGEOUS CD-ROM by using the request form on page 312.

Beyond what I can do for you is the clear conversation-piece nature of my card versus all other cards, which, as you know, are boring. You've seen business cards and you know that if you've seen one, you've seen them all. Unless of course you've seen mine. Mine is rich.

And mine is actually a foldout card that provides, on the inside, six quick selling points about what I offer. Any of these can be a trigger to action.

And so I offer a memorable card that you must keep. And when you do keep it, you find yourself looking at my selling points over and over again. "Hey," you think to yourself, "maybe I should hire Bill."

Not maybe. You should!

OUTRAGEOUS exercise

Your business card is a mini sales card. Besides the obvious pertinent information, such as name, title, business, phone number, fax, and e-mail, you want to concentrate on a number of things depending on your type of business:

1. What do you do?
2. What results do you offer?
3. What products or services do you offer?
4. What achievements have you accomplished?
5. What can you guarantee?
6. How are you different or special?
7. Why should someone choose to do business with you?

In other words, provide more than the pertinent information.

Finally, list some OUTRAGEOUS ways to design your business card so that it gets noticed and kept. Think in terms of:

- shape
- color
- paper stock
- graphic design

stand out or get thrown out!

The competition for attention is intense. As a consumer, you know that, and you know what gets your attention.

Facts are hard to ignore, and the facts are these:

- People are bored.
- People are overwhelmed.
- People like to be amused.

You can be like everybody else and be treated like everybody else. Or you can be OUTRAGEOUS.

Think about the biggest day for advertisers in America—the Super Bowl. What happens? People watch the biggest football game of the year, and they watch the commercials. Why is everyone interested in the commercials? Because they are OUTRAGEOUS, and people love OUTRAGEOUS advertising!

You can be OUTRAGEOUS without spending Super Bowl money. People will love you, and you'll earn super money!

7 steps to apply OUTRAGEOUS advertising in your business, career, and your life

Step #1
Grasp the concept that all advertising can be OUTRAGEOUS.

You don't have to be boring. You can actually stand out no matter what you do and in what media you do it.

For instance, cited in this chapter are examples of OUTRAGEOUS advertising by dressing up in a costume, in help-wanted ads, on rack cards, in magazine ads, on window signs, in radio ads, in direct mail, and even on business cards. Throughout this book is proof that you can successfully use OUTRAGEOUS advertising everywhere.

Step #2
Understand that you are NOT your customer.

After I deliver a seminar on OUTRAGEOUS advertising, there is always somebody who approaches me with, "Bill, I love your kind of advertising, but it won't work in my business because my customers (or clients or patients or prospects) are too sophisticated for that kind of advertising."

While I seldom get into a heated discussion over it, they are typically dead wrong because people are bored and overwhelmed and often the only way to cut through the clutter is to be OUTRAGEOUS. Who notices? Everyone. And if they notice, they are much more likely to buy. This type of advertising appeals to all types of customers from all walks of life.

If it's appealing and interesting, it's plenty sophisticated. I've had presidents of Fortune 1000 companies, presidents of banks, accountants, and lawyers respond to OUTRAGEOUS advertising. And they've done so with enthusiasm. These are some of the same people who many think would never respond to this type of advertising because it isn't "sophisticated" enough for them.

Remember, you are not your customer (and besides, you like this type of advertising too or else you wouldn't be reading this book!).

Step #3
Train your brain to look for ideas in "obvious" places.

Advertising is everywhere. All you have to do is look around. This step essentially says to pay attention to other advertisements and trends and to think of ways to make them fit OUTRAGEOUSLY into a campaign of your own.

By training yourself to notice what others regard as clutter, you may find a sliver of an idea in something that doesn't look like an idea at all. For instance, in chapter 4, you'll read of my diner placemat mailer that I created for my menswear stores. This idea came to me when I was sitting in a diner having dinner with my wife and the placemat itself was an advertisement for the diner. But I saw it as something more.

56

The truth is you can receive inspiration for your OUTRAGEOUS advertising in just about anything that you encounter in your everyday life if you train yourself to constantly be on the lookout for it.

Step #4

Train your brain to look for ideas in "unobvious" places.

If you are on the lookout at all times, you sometimes stumble upon a great OUTRAGEOUS idea. I find this is especially true whenever I travel.

For instance, I thought of ideas for creating OUTRAGEOUS advertising while I was riding a donkey in Santorini, Greece, and riding a camel in the Negev Desert in Israel. Both of these examples are used in this book."

Even when you think you are completely removed from your business, you can still find opportunities to create OUTRAGEOUS advertising.

Step #5

Get involved in the OUTRAGEOUS campaign.

You as a personality can take the lead in your OUTRAGEOUS campaign. You can position your business, your products and services, and yes, even yourself in an OUTRAGEOUS manner that will get noticed.

So consider ways to get involved. Personal involvement when done right really does increase business.

Step #6

Swipe and deploy (S&D).

This concept is so powerful that I wrote an entire chapter (chapter 10) about it titled: "**S**wiping Ideas and **D**eploying Them into Your Business." What does this mean? It means that even if you don't consider yourself creative or able to find ideas in which to apply OUTRAGEOUS advertising as I suggest in steps #3 and #4 above, you can S&D (swipe and deploy) them from others.

Frankly, that's one of the big benefits of this book. I give you stuff to swipe and deploy.

This book is, in fact, full of proven and successful OUTRAGEOUS advertising that are ready to be S&D'd for your own business. All you have to do is swipe the ones that work for you, tweak the copy for your own purpose, and get it out. That's how easy applying OUTRAGEOUS advertising is.

<u>Step #7</u>
Discover that OUTRAGEOUS advertising is FUN.

Have fun.

One of the biggest bonuses to applying OUTRAGEOUS advertising is that it's simply fun to do. You'll find out very shortly after you apply it that your customers love it. You'll also find it to be the most enjoyable thing you do in your business (with the possible exception of making more income, which the OUTRAGEOUS advertising brings to you).

But it's true. This kind of advertising is fun. This was true in my retail menswear stores, and it's still true in my Glazer-Kennedy Insider's Circle marketing company. Sure, my customers and now members are always looking forward to the next piece of OUTRAGEOUS advertising that comes from me, but I really have fun creating it.

I no longer think of how much money I make. I don't have to. I just know that by applying OUTRAGEOUS advertising, I will be OUTRAGEOUSLY successful—and so will you.

Sizzling Outrageous Summation

1) OUTRAGEOUS works. Why it does is irrelevant. It does.

2) OUTRAGEOUS works in any media for any product.

3) People are bored and overwhelmed, and want to be amused.

4) People love OUTRAGEOUS advertising.

5) Always be on the lookout for the next OUTRAGEOUS idea.

6) Discover that OUTRAGEOUS advertising is the number-one most fun thing you'll do in your career.

4) Using The Most Powerful Tool — Direct Mail

One night after work, my wife, Karen, and I decided to stop at a local diner and grab a quick dinner. We ordered our meal, and my wife began to give me ... "The list!"

What's the list?

Well, if you've been married as long as I have, you'll probably relate to this! She was giving me a list, you know, a Honey-do list. Do this, do that, do ... Wait, wait ...

The list was so long that I needed something to write on so I wouldn't forget the list. I had a pen in my pocket but no paper to write on. After looking around, the only paper I saw was a placemat in front of me on the table.

If you've ever noticed a placemat in a diner, you know that it is usually filled up with advertisements about the diner, or they sell advertising space to other local businesses.

This placemat was no different, but there was a one-inch blank border that went around the placemat. Ah! Blank space. So I carefully and meticulously tore off one side of the blank space, and I wrote very ... very ... very small and I made the list.

Then guess what happened? I realized that you could write something on a placemat, and the light bulb in my head went off. I figured out that writing a sales message on a placemat and mailing it out to people would be a really cool idea.

So the idea for my placemat mailing was actually born right in a diner of all places!!!

OUTRAGEOUS exercise

Make a list of all of the places you frequent that can inspire you to think up ideas to create OUTRAGEOUS advertising. This might sound a bit tricky, but once you give this a little bit of thought, it's not as hard as you might think.

1.

2.

3.

Now, back to my placemat mailer. One of the things you'll learn when you do OUTRAGEOUS advertising—and you'll hear me say it several times throughout this book—is that this kind of advertising can be fun. In fact, as you create more and more OUTRAGEOUS advertising, you'll find that it will get your creative juices flowing and will probably become the most enjoyable (and profitable) thing that you do in your business.

Let me show you what I mean with my placemat.

Since I created this placemat, I figured I had complete control of what it looked like. So, as you can see on my placemat, I created a fictitious diner that I called "FAT EDDIE'S," which is open 24/7 and features home-cooked meals.

Bill Glazer's placemat mailing. *You can see this in full color when you claim your FREE CD of all of the exhibits in this book by using the form on page 312.*

In addition, at the bottom of my placemat I included what we provide, which is:

- breakfast
- lunch
- dinner
- desserts
- cocktails

AND …

- lap dances!!!!

Obviously, I tend to get a bit creative with OUTRAGEOUS advertising … and you can have fun with it too.

I wasn't done yet. I wanted to make it even more OUTRAGEOUS, so I also printed on the front of the placemat a simulated coffee stain with a handwritten note that read:

"Sorry about the coffee stain, but all I had to write on was this stupid placemat here at the Diner where I was having breakfast... Anyway, just open this up right now.... You won't believe what I'm going to offer you on the inside... Bill"

Then I folded it up, had it tabbed to meet the post office requirement, put on a first-class live stamp, and took it to the post office.

Bill Glazer's placemat *ready to put into the mail complete with simulated coffee stain. You can see this in full color when you claim your FREE CD of all of the exhibits in this book by using the form on page 312 .*

Hopefully you are now seeing why I sent a placemat mailer instead of putting my sales message in an envelope like everybody else. I did it because it gets noticed.

Think about it. If your sales message arrives in the big pile of mail that's in the mailbox every day and looks like everybody else's sales message, it doesn't get noticed. It just doesn't.

But, if it arrives on a placemat …

64

You think, "What the heck is this?" and then you see a coffee stain on it and the curiosity forces you to stop and say, "Hey, I've got to see what this is all about." If it arrives on a placemat, the message DOES GET NOTICED.

There's more to say about the placemat mailer and why it worked. But first, I'd like to say a few words about my favorite type of OUTRAGEOUS advertising—direct mail.

why use direct mail?

First of all, you want to use direct mail because everyone gets mail. Not everyone owns a television or listens to a radio or buys a newspaper or owns a computer, but since everyone gets mail, everyone is reachable.

Plus, everyone looks at direct mail. In fact, studies have shown that looking through your big pile of mail is one of the first things that people do when they get home from work. (It's right up there with going to the bathroom.)

And for that reason, direct mail is my favorite medium for advertising, and especially for OUTRAGEOUS advertising. Precisely because it is easy to fade into the middle of a pile of mail, it's also easy to stand out. So much of all of our mail just fades away. But if you stand out, you will get read.

And by getting read, you can really write. The old sales adage of "the more you tell, the more you sell" is especially true with direct mail, which offers the added bonus of no space or time limitations. I've written sales letters forty-eight pages long, and I've found them to be effective.

Of course, everyone also throws out a lot of mail unopened or barely glanced at, but that's not a reason not to use mail. It's just part of the challenge … and of the opportunity.

The fact remains that we are all trained to go through our mail every single day, and we separate it into three different piles. I call them the A pile, the B pile, and the C pile (see chapter 2).

Of course, getting into people's mailboxes is easy. What you really want to do is get in the right mailboxes—those of people who would welcome your message and are likely to respond to it. So, let's talk about whose mailbox you want your mail to arrive in.

who wants <u>YOUR</u> mail?

There are basically three different groups of people whose mailboxes you want to go after.

Group #1: YOUR CURRENT CUSTOMERS

The first group, and the one that is most likely to find your mail interesting, is your current customers/clients/patients. These are people who have done business with you in the past, who already know you and hopefully trust you.

And so, provided that they had a good experience with you previously, this group will be the most responsive to your marketing messages.

But to reach them requires you to do one of the most important things that you can do for your business—create your own customer list.

Obviously, this can be done quite easily with any good CRM (customer relationship management) software system that will house your customer list. Once you decide to create your own database, you need to decide what information you want to put in it.

OUTRAGEOUS boost

A great advantage of creating a database of your customers is that it becomes an important asset of your business. For example, if you ever decide to sell your business, a database of all of your customers will make it worth considerably more to the buyer.

Typically you always want to put in the basics, which include:

- Name
- Address
- Phone number
- E-mail
- Street address

And then you want to include any other information that will help you make good decisions about when to contact them with your marketing messages.

This will often include things such as:

- What was bought
- When purchases are made
- How the customer buys (for example, during sales or at regular price)
- The customer's birthday
- The customer's anniversary

As you can imagine, this type of information becomes absolutely priceless to you when deciding how to market to your customers.

OUTRAGEOUS exercise

Make a list of all of the information that you want to track in your customer database and that you need in order to make good decisions about when and how to advertise to them. This is perhaps one of the most important and valuable things you will ever do for your business.

It takes time to build a good list of your customers, but it is worth it. Your customers are your most valuable assets. Period. And if you don't have a customer list, you should begin assembling one immediately. Once you begin to collect information, you will inevitably learn things about your business that will surprise you and eventually become priceless.

Group #2: GENERATED LISTS SIMILAR TO YOUR LIST

The second group of people you want to mail to are those people who are as similar as possible to those on your own customer list. Which is another reason you want to carefully create your own customer list.

Why is this?

Well, I'm sure you've heard of the old adage that "birds of a feather flock together." This means that people who are just like your own customers also behave just like them, so they are more likely to do business with you than people who are not like your own customers.

Now we are getting into buying lists of people who are as similar to your own customer list as possible. In order to do this, you need to have your current customer list profiled.

Send your list off to a list broker and have them run your list through their software in order to look for commonalities in it that will help you make smart list-buying decisions.

For example, you probably want to see things such as:

- The percent of male versus female customers
- The areas where most of your customers live
- The age ranges that most of your customers fall into
- The income ranges that most of your customers fall into

This list can be endless. You can find out anything you want about your customers. As Dan Kennedy says, there is no privacy in America, and anything can be found out about you.

For example, I've had clients who want to know things about their customers such as:

- What magazines they read
- How many of them are pet owners
- What percent of them are married
- What types of cars they drive
- What percent of them own a second home
- What percent of them are Republicans versus Democrats

All of this information, and much more, can be found out about your own customer list. And this will help you to identify who are the most likely people to buy from you.

OUTRAGEOUS resource

The largest list broker in the world is InfoUSA. They can profile your list and help you to identify the best lists to purchase. You can find information about them at InfoUSA.com.

OUTRAGEOUS exercise

Make a list of all of the information that you would like to know about your customers in order to make smart decisions about which lists of people you would like to test. This might take some thought, and again, a good and reputable list broker can help you with this.

OUTRAGEOUS boost

When buying a list, more is typically not better. In order to increase your response percentage, you normally want to try to narrow your list of prospects as much as possible to contain as many of the characteristics of your "best" customers. When doing a local mailing, I have typically found that 500 names is a good test. On a national level, I like to test 5,000 names. Then if you get a good ROI (return on your investment), you can always go back and buy more names.

Group #3: REFERRALS

The third group of people that you want to send mail to are referrals. In fact, referrals are the second most likely to respond to your mailings (only second to your existing customers).

Obviously the best place to get referrals from is your existing customers. The problem is that most businesses expect their customers to refer them to their friends, family members, and coworkers. But this is often not the case.

When customers don't refer others, it isn't because they are not satisfied with the products and services that you provide. Most customers simply forget to refer because they are busy. Referring your business to others is not a priority, and they probably never mention your business unless someone asks them if they know someone who provides what you sell. Then, you may get a referral. Otherwise, when you are out of sight, you are most likely also out of mind.

OUTRAGEOUS resource

My Business Building Marketing System has a great Customer Rewards Referral System developed in it that works for any type of business. For information, go to bgsmarketing.com.

Therefore, it is actually your job to remind them to refer their friends to you. Just think about it. If every one of your customers would simply refer just one person, you will double your customer count and quite possibly your business.

So now that you know who gets your mail, what should you send them? Well, you can begin to try out some of the OUTRAGEOUS techniques I am about to teach you. This is fun stuff …

unusual-looking mail

Doesn't all direct mail look about the same—white envelope, impersonal typing of the addresses, and a metered stamp?

No?

DEFINITELY, NO!

The best way to get someone to stop and look at what you've sent is to get the mail opener to say, "Gee, that's unusual. Who is sending me this? I am compelled to open it."

Gathering and reading the mail is such an everyday event that the only way to stand out among all the clutter is to send something that people simply have to open. Here are a couple of my favorite examples.

We've all been to the movies and ordered an expensive bag of popcorn that just tastes better with a large screen in front of you.

Well, Rick Canfield, an owner of a rugged outdoor store that loves to do OUTRAGEOUS advertising, found a way to send an empty popcorn bag through the mail. Obviously when you get home from work and see a popcorn bag in your big pile of mail, you've got to open it up right away. This is another great example of getting into the A pile.

Rick Canfield's popcorn bag mailer. You can see this in full color when you claim your FREE CD of many of the exhibits in this book by using the form on page 312.

Actually, it wasn't empty. It was just empty of popcorn. In fact, it had a sales letter on the inside.

Rick Canfield's sales letter inside the popcorn bag mailer and ticket.
You can see this in full color when you claim your FREE CD
of many of the exhibits in this book by using the form on page 312.

genuine imitation official-looking envelope

When you get something in the mail from the government, it looks official, doesn't it? In fact, it looks important so you have to open it up right away, which places it into the important A pile.

Plus, major companies send out official-looking envelopes—especially if a big financial transaction is involved. Once again, it looks important and you have to open it up right away.

And so why wouldn't you want to get your mail in the A pile by making it look official also?

You can offer your customers a very official-looking reason to do business with you by sending out your message in an official-looking envelope.

Bill Glazer's official-looking envelope that he developed for his menswear retail stores. You can see this in full color when you claim your FREE CD of many of the exhibits in this book by using the form on page 312.

This particular official-looking envelope has a number of features including the "EXPRESS First Class Mail" printed right on the envelope. In addition, there is a tracking number complete with what appears to be a hand-checked box next to the tracking number.

Notice that the inside stationery matches the envelope. It even has the same tracking number. And because of this appearance of a reason (see chapter 1, "reason why" copy), the campaign makes sense in a very official-feeling way.

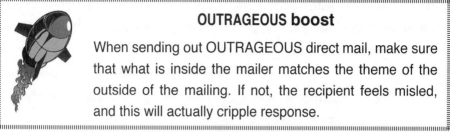

OUTRAGEOUS boost

When sending out OUTRAGEOUS direct mail, make sure that what is inside the mailer matches the theme of the outside of the mailing. If not, the recipient feels misled, and this will actually cripple response.

Who is sending me this? I am compelled to open it.

wallet mailer

Ever get a wallet in the mail?

Well, if you did, you'd have to open it, wouldn't you? After all, what's inside a wallet? Money!!! Who wouldn't want to see if someone was sending them money?

The wallet mailer with money protruding from the top and coupons inside. You can see this in full color when you claim your FREE CD of many of the exhibits in this book by using the form on page 312.

I have used these wallet mailers for many of my clients and my own businesses, and always with huge success. Heck, I even used them one year for my menswear stores when I hired college students to hand them out in busy areas that got a lot of pedestrian traffic during the busy Christmas shopping season.

I've always included a sales letter or a couple of money-savings coupons inside of them. One technique that gets a big boost in response is to print what appears to be real money at the top of the insert sticking out just a little bit from the top of the wallet mailer. That gets it opened in a hurry.

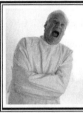

OUTRAGEOUS resource

Information about the wallet envelope mailer is available at www.walletmailer.com.

invitation mailer

You are invited to …

When you get an invitation in the mail, don't you want to immediately know what you're invited to? Of course you do. So if you get an invitation in the mail, you will open it.

This particular invitation is a tri-folded mailer on 8½" by 14" paper that looks like a real invitation with a gold foil sticker "RSVP" on the outside.

Just about any business can use this as a relatively inexpensive OUTRAGEOUS mailing. I've used it several times for my retail stores to invite customers to a trunk show. Many entrepreneurs that I know have used it as an invitation to a seminar. Heck, I

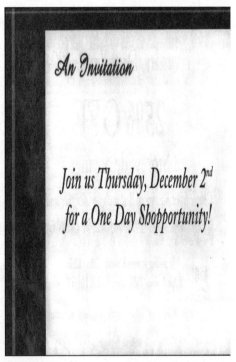

An Invitation

Join us Thursday, December 2ⁿᵈ for a One Day Shopportunity!

Invitation mailer. You can see this in full color when you claim your FREE CD of the exhibits in this book by using the form on page 312.

even know someone who owns an adult video store who used it. (I wonder what they got invited to.)

dimensional mail

Some kinds of OUTRAGEOUS advertising are more expensive than others. Typically what I refer to as dimensional mail falls into this category.

What is dimensional mail?

Well, as the name suggests, it is mail that is more than just paper. It's mail that has a thickness to it. Perhaps a better way of describing it is lumpy mail or 3-D mail.

While this type of mailing is a bit more expensive, when done correctly, it will always pay for itself. There are a couple of reasons why dimensional mail generates higher response.

First of all, this is typically what I call "top-of-the-pile" mail because there is no other choice. It doesn't fit in the pile. In fact, if there were two or three of them—whatever they are—you still probably couldn't make a pile. Dimensional mail has to be on the top of the big pile of mail that you receive every day, so it is the first thing that you see when you look at your mail.

Dimensional mail also creates a lot of curiosity, and that gets you into the A pile. When people pick up an envelope and feel something lumpy inside, it really grabs their curiosity and makes them open it up because it suggests that there's something in there that they really want.

Therefore, dimensional mail has a big advantage of being on top of the pile. Plus, dimensional mail, as a tool, screams out for some OUTRAGEOUS execution. Let me show you a couple of my favorite examples of dimensional mailings.

mini-trashcan mailing

So a little mini trashcan—about two inches tall—shows up in your mailbox one day.

It could say many things on the side. For instance: Don't throw this away. This is the opportunity of a lifetime.

OUTRAGEOUS resource

Mini-trashcan mailers are available at http://www. OUTRAGEOUS-advertising.com/3DMailings/.

A trashcan delivered to your mailbox can send a very powerful OUTRAGEOUS message. I have very seldom seen a business that couldn't use this to deliver some derivation of the message: YOU'RE THROWING AWAY AN OPPORTUNITY TO (FILL-IN-THE-BLANK).

This is a great thing to send to anyone in the mail, and there are many fun ways to play with the wording. But a trashcan in the mail?

Who is sending me this? I am compelled to open it.

Glazer-Kennedy Insider's Circle letter crumpled up and mailed inside a mini trashcan. You can see this in full color when you claim your FREE CD of many of the exhibits in this book by using the form on page 312.

For example, on this page is a letter my marketing company (Glazer-Kennedy Insider's Circle) crumpled up and sent in a mini trashcan to everyone who attended one of our seminars but did not register to attend next year's event.

coconut mailing

Honey, I got the mail. There was a tax bill, a phone bill, a letter from your mother, and a coconut.

79

If you received all of these in the mail, which one do you think you'd open first? I betcha the coconut!

Seriously, you can send a simulated coconut through the mail, and if you do, it's the first thing that will be opened. Check it out.

You can see this in full color when you claim your FREE CD of many of the exhibits in this book by using the form on page 312.

What theme could you use when you mail a coconut? Well, the theme I've usually used is some derivation of "YOU'D BE NUTS NOT TO TAKE ADVANTAGE OF THIS OPPORTUNITY."

OUTRAGEOUS resource

Simulated zipper-up coconut mailers are available at Impact Products (www.impactproducts.net).

the tube mailer

Now we're moving into making your dimensional mailer a bit more targeted. In fact, this is one of those targeted mailing list concepts that bring together (as much of this book does) a bunch of ideas into one great campaign.

Actually, the tuxedo tube is just one OUTRAGEOUS part of a sequential campaign (see chapter 9) that I targeted to high school senior boys in need of a tuxedo for their upcoming prom.

If a seventeen- or eighteen-year-old boy comes home and finds a tuxedo tube in the mail with his name on it, he has to open it. First of all, he probably rarely gets much mail anyway, and he certainly never gets mail like this. Plus, he does need a tux for his upcoming prom. The inside of the tube has a coupon for a tux.

The tube is so cool that he just has to keep it for a while. He'll show it to his friends—and incidentally, they all are going to the prom too (although they probably each received their own tuxedo tube). But this tube is just part of a larger campaign to reach these specific customers at a specific tux-needing time in their lives.

Tuxedo tube. *You can see this in full color when you claim your FREE CD of many of the exhibits in this book by using the form on page 312.*

OUTRAGEOUS resource

Tube mailings are available in many different themes. You can find them at www.selfsealtubes.com.

The world's biggest discount coupon, mailed inside of a tuxedo tube.
You can see this in full color when you claim your FREE CD of many of the
exhibits in this book by using the form on page 312.

In this case, the cost of the mailing is well worth it. A tuxedo tube in the mail?

Dude, who is sending me this? I gotta open it.

Now don't make the mistake of thinking that you don't rent tuxedos so you could never use this type of mailing. Heck, you can wrap a blank tube with anything. I even know a lot of entrepreneurs who mail a blank tube and get terrific results.

OUTRAGEOUS exercise

Create a headline for each of the OUTRAGEOUS mailings that I've shown you in this chapter for your business. I'll bet you can use every one of them after you give them a little bit of thought.

1. Popcorn Bag Mailing

Headline: _____

2. Official-Looking Mailing

Headline: _____

3. Wallet Mailer

Headline: _____

4. Invitation Mailing

Headline: _____

5. Mini-Trashcan Mailing

Headline: _____

6. Coconut Mailing

Headline: _____

7. Tube Mailing

Headline: _____

Now that you've created a headline for each of them, don't you want to get several of them out in the mail to your customers or prospects? You'll be glad you did!!!

Sizzling Outrageous Summation

1) OUTRAGEOUS advertising is fun to do.

2) Everyone gets mail.

3) Everyone separates their mail into three piles (A, B, and C).

4) Those on your own customer list are the best people to mail to.

5) Find lists of people who are similar to your best customers to mail to.

6) The best place to get referrals is from your own customers.

7) Unusual-looking mail gets noticed.

8) Dimensional mail rises to the top of any pile.

5) **Presenting Critical Components**

Yanik Silver's basement was cluttered when he came up with his best OUTRAGEOUS idea for a scratch-and-dent sale.

Actually, it was his wife who came up with the idea … inadvertently. His wife, Missy, told him that he needed to get rid of the clutter in his basement. Thus, an idea for an OUTRAGEOUS online campaign was born.

Yanik is a friend of mine who sells educational resources—manuals, CDs, and DVDs—that provide information to online marketers. And, well, he had a basement full of great manuals, CDs, and DVDs—except they weren't in perfect condition. Some of them had a bent corner; others had a crooked label; and some had been taken to a seminar to show as a sample. Whatever the reason, they could no longer be sold as in 100 percent perfect condition.

OUTRAGEOUS resource

Yanik Silver's contact info:
Website: https://surefiremarketing.com
Phone: 301-770-0423

But the information that was contained in them was still in perfect condition and still very valuable. Unfortunately, they had accumulated over time and had filled up an entire big closet in his basement. So

Yanik decided to try a new kind of campaign to get rid of them ... an OUTRAGEOUS campaign.

Yanik, you see, is a great marketer, and we often share ideas back and forth. But at this one point, he simply outdid himself. Again, it was an idea grounded in truth. And it was a sequential campaign (see chapter 9).

First, he sent an e-mail asking his readers to simply do one thing: "I need your help to put me back into good graces with my wife."

Check out the e-mail below:

```
[[firstname]], save Yanik's marriage sale...

Hi [[firstname]],

I need your help to put me back into good graces with my wife.

Last night when I heard the yelling from the basement I knew I
was in trouble. Big trouble.

    "Y - - A - - N - - I - - K!!  Get down here NOW!"

Oh oh...

I came downstairs and in my sweetest, most innocent voice I
asked, "Yes honey, what's up?"...

Missy pointed to our... (to be continued)

* * *

You can find out the rest of this story along with
pictures of my 'big mess' right here:

http://www.surefiremarketing.com/saveyanik/

I sure hope you can help.

Best,

Yanik Silver

P.S. Get over there now because my screw-up is actually
your BIG opportunity to save on some of our best-selling
products and resources. You'll find out the whole scoop
here:

http://www.surefiremarketing.com/saveyanik/
```

Yanik Silver's e-mail promoting his "SAVE YANIK'S MARRIAGE" Sale.
You can see this in full color when you claim your FREE CD of many
of the exhibits in this book by using the form on page 312.

Yanik's wife really did want his basement cleared of clutter. This is absolutely true. So Yanik, being an OUTRAGEOUS-thinking entrepreneur, sent out this e-mail, which linked to a Web page containing a sales letter. This now allowed him to tell his entire story.

Yanik Silver's sales letter promoting his "SAVE YANIK'S MARRIAGE" Sale.
You can see this in full color when you claim your FREE CD of
the exhibits in this book by using the form on page 312.

I love how this was a wild and memorable campaign that got attention and was OUTRAGEOUS plus OUTRAGEOUSLY successful. In fact, the sales letter sold everything that was in Yanik's basement. I also love how it illustrates essential direct-response elements.

OUTRAGEOUS **boost**

Yanik used a reason why he was having a sale—to save his marriage. As I mentioned in chapter 1, this is called "reason why" copy, and it will always increase response because it makes your sale much more believable.

Think about it. Isn't it better than just saying you're having a sale?

Below is an example of how Yanik has used "reason why" copy to create other sales:

"Scratch & Dent" sale

"Fire/Flood" sale

"Need to pay my taxes" sales

Birthday or anniversary sale

"My server crashed" sale

"It's raining out" sale

"Boss is away" sale, etc., etc.

Look at the online advertisement again.

It works because Yanik used a lot of really great direct-response tools, but it also has what I have identified as three essential direct-response elements:

- A HEADLINE
- AN OFFER
- A DEADLINE

There is obviously a headline—an OUTRAGEOUS headline.

Help "Save Yanik's Marriage" Sale

That makes you interested, and the photo makes it believable, and then there is the offer:

"Instead of just trashing these products or sending them back to the supplier (and letting them profit), I've decided to offer them to you at a significant discount."

And a deadline. In this case, the deadline is not a date but the limited quantity of the items he has available:

"I suggest you act fast… the deals are only around until we run out of each item."

Yanik Silver is a master marketer who has learned many tricks of the trade including the various ways to present direct-response elements. But he knows that it is important to include—and NEVER leave out—any of the three essential direct-response elements because together they cause recipients of your ads to respond.

In fact, each of the three essential direct-response elements can't really stand alone. They must always be present and used together.

In Yanik's case, they very effectively helped Yanik do exactly what he needed to—clean out his clutter. Of course Yanik's marriage wasn't really in trouble, but that doesn't matter because no one reading it would actually think that anyway. However, seeing the clutter gives you a sense of how Yanik's wife might feel about all his accumulated stuff.

Yet it needed more than a photo to tell the story.

OUTRAGEOUS exercise

Create an event for your own business using "reason why" copy like Yanik did for his "SAVE YANIK'S MARRIAGE" Sale. For example, this is perfect for any time things are slow in your business, you've hit a milestone in your business (or personal life), or you need to get rid of inventory.

Now let's take a more in-depth look at the three essential direct-response elements.

essential direct-response element #1: *headlines*

The headline is the most important part of any advertisement. It is often referred to as the advertisement to the advertisement. Think about it. When you are skimming a newspaper, magazine, Web site, direct mail piece, etc., what's the first thing you look at? The headline, of course! It's the thing that will either grab your attention and make you find out more about the ad or cause you to say to yourself, "Not interested," and move on.

A great headline needs to answer one (or all) of the following:

- Who cares?
- What's in it for ME?
- Why are you bothering me?
- So what?

For example, here's an example of a bad headline:

"50% OFF SALE"

The above headline doesn't really answer any of the four questions on our list above, plus it's boring and overused. Now here's an example of how I took the message of the headline above and turned it into a very good headline for a furniture store:

"Who Else Wants to QUICKLY & EASILY Discover How You Can Save HALF OFF On All Your Furniture Purchases Before April 27th?"

Of course there's nothing wrong with getting OUTRAGEOUS with your headlines and having a little fun with them. Here's an example of how I took the same message and created an OUTRAGEOUSLY successful headline:

"Oh Momma – get out the smelling salts!! When you find out you can buy all of your furniture at HALF PRICE from now until April 27th, the shock will probably send you right into a dead faint."

Which one of the above three headlines do you think earned the best response?

Of course, the third one got the best response. After all, it's OUTRAGEOUS!!!

OUTRAGEOUS boost

When writing headlines, don't just jump at the first one that you think of. When writing a marketing piece, I will never write less than ten headlines. I have written as many as 100 headlines before I have chosen one I wanted to use.

Therefore, the headline is your first impression and maybe your only impression unless you get it right. So get it right. Getting someone to say, "Gee, I want to read the rest" is the goal of the headline.

headlines for all kinds of advertising

If it's an advertisement of any kind, it needs a headline. It doesn't just have to be a direct mail piece, magazine ad, newspaper ad, or a Web page. It can be a billboard, a sign in your business, a radio ad, or any kind of media for that matter.

Let's look at a radio advertisement for example. The headline needs to be the very first thing that you hear. Although it's not in print so you can see it, it's the headline. It's the thing that makes you stop and say to yourself, "I have to listen to the rest of this," the same way that a headline in print has to make you want to read the rest of it.

OUTRAGEOUS resource

Whenever I am stumped on an idea or just to get my brain moving, I look at a list of 350 of the best headlines ever written. These are great to turn into templates and create your own headlines. They serve as an OUTRAGEOUS shortcut. In appendix A, I've filtered down my list and given you my favorite 100 that you can use to make your own templates.

OUTRAGEOUS exercise

Below are some of the most common headline templates that I have used over the years. Fill in the blanks for your business to create some winning headlines.

Headline Template #1:

_____ That Other _____

Don't Want You to Know About

Headline Template #2:

Discover the Secret of _____ and

Slash Your _____ in _____

Headline Template #3:

If You _____, You'll Love Our _____

Headline Template #4:

Remember When You Could Have_____

and Didn't

Headline Template #5:

Want to Save a Bundle? An Open Letter to Everyone
Who_____

Headline Template #6:

Would You Buy a _____ for _____?

essential direct-response element #2: *the offer*

People will only respond to your advertisement for one of two reasons: either fear of loss or personal gain. What does this mean?

Well, either they will lose out by not responding or they will gain something by responding. When crafting your offer, you always want to ask yourself the following question:

"What will my prospects or customers lose if they don't respond or gain if they respond to my offer?"

This is a critical concept that will help you immensely when crafting an offer. Now don't think that you always have to sell at a discount when crafting your offer as Yanik did with his "SAVE YANIK'S MARRIAGE" Sale.

While most people tend to offer a discount when conducting a sale, this is not always necessary. For example, think about when Nike introduces a new shoe. Nobody sells them initially at a discount. All they have to do is advertise that a new supply will be arriving on Tuesday, and people will stand in line all night for the chance to buy a pair at whatever price.

This is a great example of a "fear-of-loss" offer.

OUTRAGEOUS **boost**

When constructing an offer, fear-of-loss will typically outperform personal gain.

essential direct-response element #3: *deadlines*

I'm going to reveal to you something about myself. I'm a procrastinator. I will ALWAYS put off until tomorrow what I don't have to do today.

Guess what else? So are you. Yes, YOU'RE a procrastinator.

How do I know?

I know because just about every person is a procrastinator. That's human nature. And that, quite simply, is why deadlines were invented.

In fact, my friend and professional copywriter John Carlton says that if it weren't for deadlines, nothing would ever get done.

So every ad that you send out must always have a deadline in order to get people to take action. While there are many ways to have deadlines, there are two that are most commonly used.

The first one is a deadline by a specific date or time. In order to take advantage of the offer, you must respond by a certain date.

The other one is a deadline by limited quantity. For example, as I mentioned above, this is the kind of deadline that Yanik used in his "SAVE YANIK'S MARRIAGE" Sale. There were only a limited number of items in the closet in his basement.

I like to use both of these deadlines in my OUTRAGEOUS advertising, and I've been even known to combine both of them to put added pressure on "us" procrastinators.

Here are two more important points about deadlines:

- When using a deadline by date, you have to be very careful not to give people too long to respond.
- When using a deadline by limited quantity, be careful not to appear to have too large of quantity available.

Remember, if the procrastinators—that's everyone—think there's no hurry in responding, they won't hurry. They will probably just figure they have a lot of time or there's plenty there … and probably never take advantage of your offer.

OUTRAGEOUS boost

My rule for deadlines by time is: when possible never give people more than two weeks to respond. I know this rule needs to be broken at times depending on the circumstance, but when possible it's a great rule to follow.

For example, years ago I did some consulting with a menswear chain that was owned by a father and his two sons.

When I first looked at their advertisements, I noticed that their deadlines were approximately two months long and were hidden in their ads with what I call four-point invisible type. This is type that's so small that you can easily miss it, and if you do notice it, you'd have to have a magnifying glass to read it.

On my insistence, they reluctantly agreed to test a two-week deadline for their offers and put the deadlines in their headlines. This made all of the difference in the world. We made the exact same offer as before, but now their customers had to respond quickly or would lose out.

Conversely, a furniture store owner who has been to several of my seminars uses deadlines of only four hours in his stores, generating hundreds of thousands of dollars in response. Talk about creating a sense of urgency. Once the word got out, the people showed up ready to buy.

Some of the very best promotions that I ran in my menswear stores were only for four days. Forcing a procrastinator to take action is always a good idea.

Now, let me show you a couple of examples of how these three essential direct-response elements work together.

the gage million-dollar-bill mailer

One thing that gets interest is money—especially the image of a "million bucks."

So one year at my menswear store, we sent out a letter with a headline asking, "Who Else Wants to Look Like a MILLION BUCKS? … And slash their wardrobe costs IN HALF!"

Plus we printed a million-dollar bill at the top of the letter.

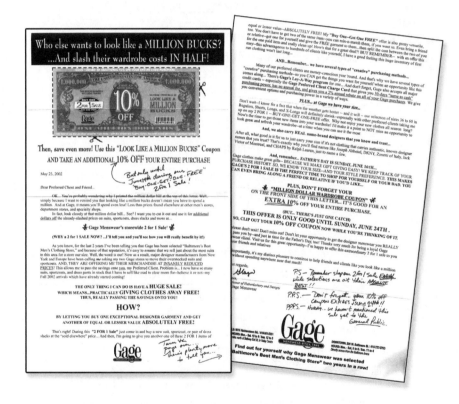

You can see this in full color when you claim your FREE CD of the exhibits in this book by using the form on page 312.

Obviously, the combination of a HEADLINE with a big promise and the visual of a million-dollar bill will cause you to stop and see what this is all about. So, the headline—the ad for the ad—did its job.

Now the OFFER is an additional 10 percent OFF YOUR ENTIRE PURCHASE, and you are first introduced to it right up in the subhead. This is important. It's best when it's easy to find and you don't have to search for it.

Finally the DEADLINE is in handwritten font right below the offer. Once again, you don't want to hide the deadline and make people have to search for it.

OUTRAGEOUS boost

Repeat the offer and deadline several times in your OUTRAGEOUS advertising to reinforce them.

canfield's sporting goods advertorial

My favorite type of newspaper ad to run is an advertorial. This is an ad deliberately designed to look like news or something from the editorial department.

In fact, here's a dirty little secret that the newspapers don't want you to know. Advertorials, when properly and cleverly written, will typically receive triple the readership of newspaper and magazine display ads.

The reason advertorials receive triple readership is that people buy newspapers and magazines for news, and advertorials look just like news.

The best marketers understand this. Jack Canfield, who owns a sporting goods store in Omaha, Nebraska, certainly understands. Jack is a serious student of OUTRAGEOUS advertising, having studied both Dan Kennedy and myself for many years. He creates great OUTRAGEOUS advertising.

So when Angie Michaels, who designs her own exclusive line of fishing gear—FISHHER—for women, was on a tour bringing her line of gear to a sporting goods store in Omaha, Nebraska, Jack's store ran an OUTRAGEOUS advertorial promoting her appearance.

You can see this in full color when you claim your FREE CD
of the exhibits in this book by using the form on page 312.

Immediately, you see what appears to be an actual newspaper story—especially from the layout and the appearance of the headline and photo.

Examining the ad closer, you see that the HEADLINE really mimics a real newspaper's headline, so it will grab your attention.

It reads:

Frustrated Female Angler Lands
Big Idea by Offering Fishing Products
and Accessories Just for Women

Let's face it; if you're a female who likes to fish, you have to read on. This ad does a great job of "flagging" the ideal person to read this right away.

So what's the OFFER? After all, there's no discount of her products, is there?

No!

Her offer is the opportunity to see ALL of her thirty products that she manufactures—all at one time. This is a great example of making an offer without discounting.

Of course the DEADLINE should be obvious. She will only be appearing in person one day (April 28th) and for only five hours (11 a.m. to 4 p.m.).

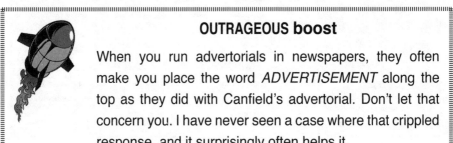

OUTRAGEOUS boost

When you run advertorials in newspapers, they often make you place the word *ADVERTISEMENT* along the top as they did with Canfield's advertorial. Don't let that concern you. I have never seen a case where that crippled response, and it surprisingly often helps it.

the automotive training institute advertorial

The Automotive Training Institute (ATI) is the largest provider of business coaching services in the U.S. for independently owned auto repair shops. They use several methods to get new clients including direct mail, telemarketing, tele-seminars, and magazine ads. They also use advertorials.

When I first began working with them, they were buying quite a few full-page ads in their industry trade magazines. None of them were generating any appreciable kind of response, and they certainly weren't paying for themselves.

After I looked at them, the answer of why they weren't working was obvious. Their ads looked like all of the other ads in magazines. In other words, brand-building ads … Ughh!!!

So, I wrote several ads for them. Of course they were my favorite kind of magazine ads—advertorials.

First I interviewed several of their clients and received some great information about how each of their own auto repair businesses grew from the coaching they were receiving from ATI.

The ads actually were a long-form testimonial, which you'll be learning a lot more about in chapter 7.

When I delivered my first advertorial to Chris "Chubby" Frederick, the owner of ATI, he showed it to many of the key people in his organization, and they all hated it.

He later told me that when he heard they hated it, he knew it was a winner.

OUTRAGEOUS boost

Be careful of choosing the wrong advisors. In other words, just because you get advice doesn't mean it is good advice. Often the people who work with you are well meaning, but they just don't know better. Dan Kennedy says that the only vote that really counts is that of the customer who is giving you money. Politely ignore all others.

On the following page is the advertorial that I wrote for ATI.

Clearly the first thing that jumps at you in this ad is the HEADLINE.

EXPOSED.

Now I didn't create this headline; I first saw it used nearly ten years ago in an ad that Dan Kennedy wrote. I'm not sure if he first created it; it doesn't matter. The only thing that matters is that it works.

What's the first thing that comes to your mind when you first see this headline and the subhead beneath it that reads:

Auto Repair Shop Owner Speaks Out and Reveals the Raw Truth About That

EXPOSED.

Auto Repair Shop Owner Speaks Out and Reveals the Raw Truth About That "Management Consultant," Chubby Frederick, Who Advertises in This Magazine All the Time.

This guy, Chubby Frederick, promises all sort of things to us auto repair shop owners- management strategies for our shops that he "promises" really pay off. Strategies to increase car count by 33%. Ways to increase the average repair order. How to combat the low cost competition and so on. Every time I read one of his ads, I thought, "Who could be dumb enough to fall for this guy's rap?" Now, I'm going to tell you the raw truth about this guy and his 'management secrets.'

My name is Steve Craven, I live in Northern Virginia with my wife and five children. I went to college in Pennsylvania and became a guitar teacher – rock star 'wanna be' for two years. I went to work in the family business in 1978 and my father died in 1980. I had no training for the business, the estate was in disarray, no one was in charge and there were many issues. By the grace of God, we some how expanded to 8 locations.

Even though I had 8 stores, I didn't really know what I was doing. I knew Chubby for over 20 years but not as a consultant. I needed to increase profits and reduce stress but couldn't seem to change anything. I registered my 5 managers, CFO and myself thinking it might be a good idea to be a little more open minded about new and different ideas. But, I still had every intention of sitting through it all day and asking for a refund. After all, after 20 years in this business, what the heck could this "Chubby" guy teach me?

What we discovered at Chubby's seminar actually scared me – most of it was so different from what we had ever seen, heard, been taught, or believed. As we listened to Chubby's information, we saw a whole different way to develop a high income business rather than just chase a job here, a job there. We saw integrity, service, smart targeted marketing, and freedom from cheapest price, roll around in the mud, bait-n-switch ugliness. Best of all, we learned actual systems to reengineer our business. I even looked in the mirror and saw Steve Craven differently. So, skeptical and grateful at the same time, we left the seminar with a workbook full of ideas.

The next day I began to implement six different Chubby Frederick strategies. Over the next couple of weeks, as we got them up and running, they all surpassed our greatest expectations. Let me give you an idea of what I am talking about.

Our first full year of implementing Chubby's strategies was 2003. That year our annual profits went from $250,000 to over $800,000 and are on target to hit

Steve Craven

$1,500,000 in net profit this year. There are more benefits for employees, I doubled the 401K, morale is up and I have more free time to give to my family and charities. I am picking up a new Saratoga airplane and thanks to Chubby, I just purchased my wife's dream home and we get to visit our beach house in Nags Head, NC much more frequently.

How, you ask, could such a thing happen? The answer, simply, is learning how real proven and effective management systems work, from the "master", Chubby Frederick. In spite of everything you hear about car counts being lower, my business is booming. One of Chubby's strategies alone delivers four to seven new customers every week ...over $1,300 per shop every week just from new customers (and it cost just a few bucks) – thanks to Chubby's systems, inspiration and encouragement.

What is important is that Steve Craven can get as many new customers as he wants, get plenty of referrals, is unaffected by competition and has 'real' systems in place to realize at least a big 20% plus bottom line profit on every job. I knew this man had it figured out when he taught me his 39 Key Performance Indicators. He is brilliant. None of us had been to school to learn the business, we simply learned from others and hoped they knew what they were talking about. So here's the raw truth about this Chubby Frederick guy: Unlike most of those 'pretend' experts, he is a bona fide management consultant and money-making genius, who can do anything from tweaking to transforming your business, so you not only make a lot of money, but you can make it a lot easier and more enjoyably than you can imagine. And, in my opinion, you're a fool to ignore him.

Just like me, you've seen his ads in this magazine month after month. If you

haven't responded, I don't know why. Maybe you think you're too smart and know it all like I did…**but if you're so smart, why aren't you rich and happy?** Maybe you are doing well already – but you could do better (some of Chubby's most ardent students make over a million dollars a year). Maybe you just don't want to be sold something that'll be a waste of your hard-earned money. About that you can relax, Chubby guarantees his stuff.

I've got over $800,000 reasons why you ought to investigate what Chubby has to offer. What reasons do you have NOT to look at this? And here's how easy it is: Chubby has prepared a straight-talk, detailed report – "WHAT 99% OF ALL OWNERS DON'T KNOW ABOUT AND WILL NEVER FIND OUT ABOUT MAKING A 20-30% CASH PROFIT IN THEIR AUTO REPAIR SHOP," which you can have absolutely FREE of cost or obligation. Get it, read it and decide for yourself whether or not you want to attend Chubby's next seminar coming to your area. It's that simple. To get your FREE REPORT, pick up the phone and call 1-800-880-3248. You will hear a brief, free recorded message and be able to leave your name and address, so your report can be mailed to you. Or write "report" on your business card or letterhead and pop it in the fax machine. Chubby's fax number is 301-498-9088. Either way, you will get his eye opening report rushed to you, free.

By the way, I wasn't paid even a penny or given anything to write this about Chubby. I am a tire dealership owner just like you. I did this just as a way of saying thanks to Chubby for everything he's done for me. And I am not the only person who feels this way. With your report, you'll also get a book of actual comments from some of the over 10,000+ other auto repair shop owners that he has helped. Most, like me, are now making more money, with less hassle than ever before. More business that we can handle flows in every day… profitability. All we can say is, "don't envy us. Join us".

STEVE CRAVEN
Craven Tire
Fairfax, Virginia

P.S. Please don't get my number and call me. The last thing I need is a zillion phone calls asking me about Chubby. I've said what I have to say right here. What else could you possibly need to know? Instead, call 1-800-880-3248 and ask for your FREE REPORT today. You owe it to your business!

You can see this in full color when you claim your FREE CD of the exhibits in this book by using the form on page 312.

"Management Consultant," Chubby Frederick, Who Advertises in This Magazine All the Time

You're probably thinking 60 Minutes or 20/20—where a company is being exposed for some wrongdoing.

Then you find out a client of the owner, Steve Craven—whose picture we see—is "exposing" Frederick as a consultant who really can help auto repair shop owners increase car count by 33 percent. This headline is effective in raising curiosity, especially in a newspaper or magazine format.

What's the OFFER? It's a free report entitled "WHAT 99% OF ALL OWNERS DON'T KNOW ABOUT AND WILL NEVER FIND OUT ABOUT MAKING 20-30% CASH PROFIT IN THEIR AUTO REPAIR SHOP."

Does this sound familiar? It should! The title of the free report is just another headline that's written in a way that answers one of the four headline questions that I revealed earlier in this chapter.

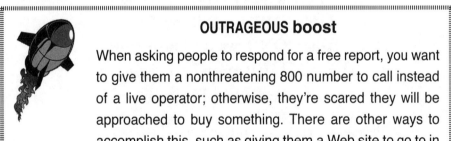

OUTRAGEOUS boost

When asking people to respond for a free report, you want to give them a nonthreatening 800 number to call instead of a live operator; otherwise, they're scared they will be approached to buy something. There are other ways to accomplish this, such as giving them a Web site to go to in order to request the free report.

Next, let's move to the DEADLINE.

The deadline? Um, uh … Where is it?

In the interest of full disclosure, I goofed. The truth is that sometimes you, like me, may not get everything perfect. And in this ad, I forgot to put in a deadline. Even though this ad was hugely successful, I'm sure it would have earned an even better response with a deadline.

In hindsight, I would have probably made the free report available to the first eighty-seven people who called, stating that ATI only printed up a very limited quantity.

the gage menswear placemat letter

Remember the placemat mailing I showed you in chapter 4? Well now I want to show you what was written on the back of the placemat that brought hundreds of customers into my stores.

When I held a sale at my retail stores, Gage Menswear, I would write headlines that tried to always go one step further. So while most stores conducted a similar type of sale like, "Rock-Bottom Prices," I wrote my HEADLINE so it really grabbed attention:

Announcing the GAGE MENSWEAR
<u>ROCK-BOTTOM PRICES</u>
FINAL REDUCTIONS SALE
You DON'T want to miss and
That OTHER men's stores won't
want you to Find out about!!

That's a headline that answers the questions I posed to you earlier in this chapter. And it does one more thing. It creates huge curiosity.

Announcing the GAGE MENSWEAR

ROCK-BOTTOM PRICES FINAL REDUCTIONS SALE
You DON'T want to miss and
That OTHER men's stores won't want you to find out about!!

(but Only until February 17th)

SORRY... please ignore the coffee stain

Dear Preferred Gage Client and Friend...

It's funny, because you never know where inspiration is gonna hit you. I'm sitting here at this diner having breakfast and going over my last inventory report... AND BANG! I realized I just had to start this sale right away... I figured it was so important that I didn't want to wait to get this typed up. So, you're getting this sale announcement in handwriting... Plus, I wanted you to know about it BEFORE I advertise it in the newspapers and on radio and TV... I have marked down our entire current season inventory up to 70% OFF!!! And, I have never marked this inventory down so low before, but I must move it out before all the new summer merchandise begins to arrive. So, come into either Gage store before February 17 and take advantage of me. PLEASE TAKE ADVANTAGE OF ME!! ...You'll actually be helping me out of a tough situation.

Here's just a brief idea of the kind of LOW prices you can expect...

① REAL Italian Suits from $158.00   ② Alexander Julian 100% Cashmere Sportcoats for just $138.00 (I must be CRAZY!)
③ Ralph Lauren Cashmere Blend Top Coats for just $138.00
④ Racquet Club 100% wool pants for just $24.99 (these are year-round weights)
⑤ 100% cotton corduroy slacks... Just $24.99 (THERE'S STILL PLENTY OF WINTER LEFT!)

And, the savings are just as good on everything throughout the stores...

PLUS... To prove to you once and for all that I absolutely, positively love my clients, just bring in this placemat before VALENTINE'S DAY and receive an additional 14-BUCKS OFF of any purchase $100.00 or more -- just shop BEFORE February 14th! (pretty clever, huh? 14-bucks off if you shop by the 14th)

Anyway, to be perfectly blunt...and at the risk of being insulting...if you miss this "Absolute ROCK-BOTTOM Final Reductions Sale, you'll cost yourself a bundle in savings and will be making a huge mistake. DROP whatever you're doing and get into GAGE NOW!!!

Best regards...

Bill Glazer

PS... Don't forget, bring in this placemat before February 14th to get an additional $14.00 OFF any purchase of $100.00 or more.

PPS... By the way, the pancakes are really good here at FAT Eddie's

You can see this in full color when you claim your FREE CD of the exhibits in this book by using the form on page 312.

OUTRAGEOUS boost

Notice in the placemat sales letter that not all of the words in the headline are treated the same. Some are capitalized; some are in all capitals; some are underlined; and others are in lowercase. That's because not all of the words are equal in importance, and they should not be treated as such. You should feature the more important words cosmetically as I've done with this headline.

Think about it. You just received a placemat in the mail with a coffee stain on it, and when you open it up, you see this letter from the owner with this curiosity-provoking headline on it.

You've just got to find out what this is all about. No wonder this was OUTRAGEOUSLY successful.

But of course we can't just stop here. It still needs to contain all three of the essential direct-response elements we've talked about in this chapter.

So, let's tackle the OFFER first. In this case, the offer is up to 70 percent OFF all current-season inventory—and then I illustrated it with five different examples.

Why did I illustrate it? Because people are very skeptical of sales, and they are suspicious of percentage discounts. They like to see what the prices are in dollars and cents.

The DEADLINE is front and center in the subhead: (but only until February 17th). The deadline is there to be seen—immediately.

OUTRAGEOUS boost

You'll notice a very cool and advanced technique in the "PS" of the placemat sales letter. There's actually a BONUS offer for quick response. I love these and use them whenever I can. It really gets people to act fast.

S.O.S.

Sizzling Outrageous Summation

1) The three crucial elements of all ads are a headline, an offer, and a deadline.

2) All ads, no matter the media, have headlines.

3) Use winning headlines as templates to create your own (see appendix for 100 best headlines list).

4) People only respond because of fear of loss or personal gain.

5) Deadlines force action…keep them as short as possible.

6) Going The Extra Mile For Extra Money

You have to be ready when an OUTRAGEOUS opportunity presents itself.

In 2002, after speaking to about 250 retailers at a seminar in Las Vegas, the editor of a major menswear magazine, MR Magazine, approached me and said he'd like to deliver my message to his readers and asked if he could do a feature on me.

Of course I did what anyone should do when presented with an opportunity to promote his or her business ... I jumped on it!

As I was standing there speaking to the editor, one of the attendees who overhead the conversation approached us and stated, "That's a great idea. Bill is out to save the retail world."

And so an idea was born. I told the editor I would love to have a story written about what I teach, but, of course, I wanted it to get noticed. So I suggested that we present it somewhat OUTRAGEOUSLY.

He quickly agreed. (Little did he know that for an opportunity to have a featured story about me I would have agreed to just about anything.)

I remembered what the retailer said about me being out to save the retail world. And the first thing that popped into my head was Superman, who was out to save the world from mass destruction.

So I decided that, for the sake of this article, I would become the Superman of Marketing.

Here's what I did. I rented a Superman costume and borrowed a pair of Clark Kent glasses from my good friend (and optometrist extraordinaire) Dr. Marc Attman, and I brought in a professional photographer to take the picture of me coming out of a phone booth, just like the real Superman.

So everything was in place except for the phone booth, which turned out to be difficult to find. So difficult, in fact, that if the real Superman were called into action today, he would be faced with a real problem. Clark Kent would probably have to go change in a bathroom stall or something in order to save the world in our modern phone booth-less times.

Finally, I found the solution at the Baltimore Museum of Industry, which has an old phone booth on display.

And it turned out great. The photo of me in a Superman costume idea took my message, which would have been displayed prominently but probably in a pedestrian manner, and made it memorable. It relays a much better story than if I am not in the outfit.

And by going the extra mile to present the message, it was effective and memorable—and it led to some great exposure for me.

And yes, I did go the extra mile … more than you'd think. Often when I show a photo during a seminar, someone walks up to me and asks about the grimace on my face in the photo.

The truth is that underneath my suit, I was wearing the entire Superman costume and those tights were so uncomfortable that … well, it really was going the extra mile.

And so my message is that there are a lot of ways to go the extra mile when you use OUTRAGEOUS advertising. After starting, of course, with a headline, an offer, and a deadline—the essential elements from chapter 5—you can do more.

You can see this in full color when you claim your FREE CD
of all of the exhibits in this book by using the form on page 312.

OUTRAGEOUS resource

I think you'll find the information that appeared in the featured article in MR Magazine very helpful to your business, regardless of what business you're in. So I've reprinted it for you in appendix C at the end of this book.

Make sure you pay close attention to "The 10 Biggest Advertising Mistakes Made by Retailers" and the 3-STEP BUSINESS BUILDING FORMULA. Just insert the category of business you're in whenever I refer to retailer.

If you really want to make money, you can take it further by paying attention to how you present your message.

OUTRAGEOUS exercise

Obviously dressing up like a superhero is not the only way you can make yourself stand out from your competition. Look at the categories below and visualize how you can present OUTRAGEOUSLY differently to convey what you or your company stands for. This is a great time to think creatively. OUTRAGEOUSLY creative!

- As a superhero
- As a rock star
- As a politician
- As a famous actor or actress
- As a famous athlete
- As a (fill-in-the-blank)

response boosters

Beyond the critical components of OUTRAGEOUS advertising, there are optional components that will enhance response even more.

While they do not have to be used every time, you'll find that when properly used, they become BIG RESPONSE BOOSTERS.

Four of the biggest response boosters that I want to concentrate on are:

- Personalization
- Double Readership Path
- Photos/Illustrations
- CopyDoodles

personalize it

Your name here!

People love to hear the sound of their own name. Not only do they like to hear it, but they also like to see it in print, and that is especially true when it comes to advertising. Your name makes you feel like someone is writing specifically to you.

Therefore, putting your customers' names in your advertising is a very smart thing and relatively easy to do today given all the "wiz-bang" equipment and software available to printers and mailing houses.

Just how smart is it?

You can increase response by as much as 30 percent by using personalization, and it typically always pays for itself.

As I suggested in chapter 4, you should already be building or acquiring (or both) a good customer list anyway, so if you have this pertinent information, why not use the one part that will generate the highest response—the person's name.

Of course, when you combine using a name with some OUTRAGEOUS techniques, it helps matters even more. For instance, let's say your name is Steve. Would you like to get mail addressed to "Dear Resident," or would you be more compelled to open something a little different?

Let me show you a great example of exactly what I mean by this, one that I used in my own retail stores.

A couple of years ago, I wanted to have an end-of-season sale for my menswear stores. Now you've probably heard of a "Buy-One-Get-One-Free" sale, but unfortunately, everybody has heard of them and they are no longer special.

Instead, I came up with an OUTRAGEOUS twist to this sale. I decided to conduct a "Buy – 1 – Get – 1 - For – 5¢" Sale. And then I gave away a nickel.

I wrote a sales letter and placed it into a 6-inch by 9-inch window envelope where the recipients could see their names from the outside. And they could also see the shiny nickel that was attached to the letter.

OUTRAGEOUS resource

You can get large window envelopes and all sorts of hard-to-find OUTRAGEOUS envelopes from www.uline.com. Nickels are available from your local bank (sorry, I couldn't help myself with the OUTRAGEOUS sarcasm about the nickel resource).

Who would send a nickel in the mail? Wouldn't someone try to steal your mail before it got to the intended recipient?

I've actually sent them a couple of times, and they always seem to arrive just fine. And when they do, they have great success.

You'll notice a few things when you look at my nickel mailing. Of course you notice the nickel and the hand-drawn arrow pointing to the nickel.

But look, it's addressed to …

STEVE

Yes, I am not just asking any random customer, but I am asking Steve himself to "DISCOVER WHY GAGE FIRST CLASS MENSWEAR IS SENDING YOU THIS?"

The elements, as you hopefully are beginning to notice, all start to fit together. OUTRAGEOUSLY!

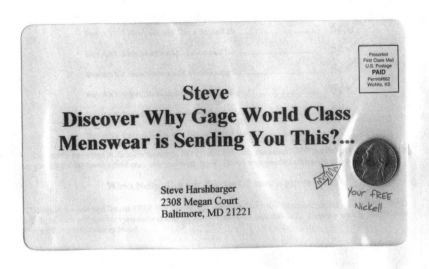

You can see this in full color when you claim your FREE CD of all of the exhibits in this book by using the form on page 312.

Notice that I used Steve's name twice in this letter. The first time was in the headline, which is the number-one most read part of any ad, and the other time was in the salutation. I often will personalize a headline because I find it really grabs the reader's attention. Using it more than once is even more effective.

OUTRAGEOUS boost

Since people's names have different numbers of letters in them, you want to always place the personalization on a separate line or at the beginning or end of the line. That way it always will fit.

Of course, salutations in a letter are also a great place to personalize since people are already used to looking for their names in a salutation.

Yet, often a salutation that you'll find in most sales letters is "Dear Friend" or "Dear Customer." I used "Dear Steve," and that is much more personal and inevitably leads to the recipient—Steve—feeling as if this letter was created just for him.

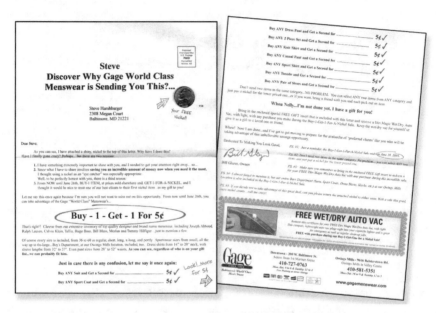

You can see this in full color when you claim your FREE CD of all of the exhibits in this book by using the form on page 312.

Personalization can be used just about anywhere, and I have seen many clever applications.

For example, Rory Fatt, who is the number-one most celebrated marketing coach, once gave away a brand-new car, and in order to advertise the giveaway, he sent out oversized postcards with a photo of the car and the recipient's name on the car's license plate. The lesson is that when you can find a place to put someone's name that makes sense, use it.

Obviously, another great place to use personalization is in e-mails. You can personalize the subject line and the salutation easily. Typically this increases response from people who will open your e-mail and read its content.

Just about any software that allows you to send out e-mails allows you to upload a file and easily personalize the e-mails for you.

From: Dan Kennedy (info@dankennedy.com)
Sent:
To:
Subject: (first name), LAST CHANCE TO SAVE $300!

Dear Bill,

A few weeks ago I sent you a special invitation to our one-of-a-kind event, the annual Info-SUMMIT. The Info-SUMMIT is NOT a run-of-the-mill seminar. As I said in previous emails, The Info-SUMMIT is a true EVENT. It is the place and time once each year when the most experienced and successful info-marketers from all over the world gather to exchange information and make deals….and generously share their business strategies with new members of this Most Unusual Millionaires Society. Nothing like it occurs anywhere else – and couldn't.

The Bad News is that there's only 48 hours left for you to register at a $300 Discount.

This is your LAST CHANCE and you'll need to hurry to secure your seat. Seating capacity is limited, and are given on a first come, first serve basis. Once they're gone, they're gone.

to get all the details click on the link below:

Linktosalesletterchoices.com

Dedicated To Multiplying Your Income,

Dan Kennedy

PS: I will even guarantee that your trip to the Info-SUMMIT proves to be one of the most fruitful trips of your entire life: if, at ANY time during the three days of the Info-SUMMIT, you honestly believe you've made a mistake and that you don't belong here or that I somehow misled you or you are otherwise disappointed, you need only say so to receive a full 100% fee refund PLUS UP TO $750.00 toward your documented travel and lodging expenses.

Linktosalesletterchoices.com

Typical e-mail with personalized subject line and salutation.

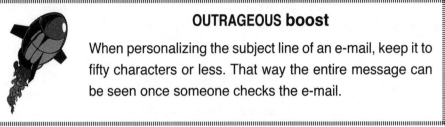

OUTRAGEOUS boost

When personalizing the subject line of an e-mail, keep it to fifty characters or less. That way the entire message can be seen once someone checks the e-mail.

double readership path

The thing that probably caught Steve's eye to begin with from the nickel mailing that I just showed you was the nickel. A nickel in the mail? That's OUTRAGEOUS.

Look again at that first page of the nickel mailer. It is not some sea of print but rather a visually enticing reach into the mind of the customer.

First, of course, there is the nickel. A nickel in the mail! Then there is a hand-drawn circle around the boldfaced offer:

"Buy – 1 – Get - 1 For 5¢"

Plus there are two different hand-drawn arrows, small print, big print, bold print, a numbered list, and a boldfaced reminder that goes onto the other side. Yes, the next side continues the message.

And the boldfaced text of:

"Buy – 1 - ... get a second for ....5¢"

And each line mentioning a different product with the same nickel deal is finished with a checkmark. But wait, there's more, and that's exactly what you see next in big bold:

"Whoa Nelly...I'm not done yet. I have a gift for you!"

Of course, between there is more print, always more for the customer to read that will help to convince him or her exactly how great this is.

But graphically, this bold phrase in the middle of the page catches your eye. And it leads to a coupon with a photo of the aforementioned free gift. (For more on gifts, see chapter 8.) And still, there is room for my signature and an italicized list of P.S. #1 through P.S. #5 that includes, of course, the deadline.

Finally, at the bottom of the second page is all the pertinent information, including the company logo, credit cards accepted, address, phone number, and Web site.

Of course, if you write a two-page sales letter (or a twenty-page or a two-paragraph letter), you must have something to say that is relevant to the customer. The words you choose and how you present them are important.

A lot of copywriting is human psychology. Knowing how the mind works, what trigger words to use, and how to present information in specific ways that cause people to buy is key.

And so when you are designing any campaign, you don't want a piecemeal approach, but instead you are going after an overall look, feel, and theme to it that makes it cohesive and also gives the pieces their individual power if they are the only parts seen.

And although this is not specifically a copywriting book, I am giving many examples featuring all the elements of good copywriting. So, for example, on the first page of the nickel mailer, you can see that it is clearly built for what professional copywriters refer to as a "double readership path."

Think about how you would read any kind of advertisement. Your eyes will scan it very quickly and determine whether or not it interests you. In the case of my nickel mailing, you'd probably notice the headline, the nickel, and a few of the other featured parts of the letter such as the handwritten font and subheads.

And by using short sentences, long sentences, and an appeal to the reader with the idea of a free gift, the letter is readable and entertaining, and it reaches many trigger points.

I just described to you the double readership path. This is the path that readers will take to see if they are interested in what you are saying to them. Then, if you grab their interest, they will read the letter in its entirety or at least until they decide whether this is for them.

OUTRAGEOUS boost

People often resist writing long-form sales letters though they will typically outperform shorter sales messages because "the more you tell, the more you sell." The double readership path allows you to write longer sales letters and capture the readers when they scan for information that grabs their attention.

Let me provide you with a couple of OUTRAGEOUS examples that illustrate the double readership path.

puzzle piece mailer

In August 2006, I helped a client, Keith Lee, put on a retail conference and expo, and as the conference was approaching, he still had a few more seats available and a list of customers he knew would be interested in attending.

He puzzled over what to do. He knew he could get a better response if he could just come up with a way to solve ...

Wait! That was it.

He would send out a puzzle piece attached to a long sales letter.

I'm Puzzled?...
Are You Absolutely Sure
Your Best Possible Decision
Is To Miss This?

Is this the winning puzzle piece?
Bring it to the Conference & EXPO to find out if
you're the winner of a Royal Carribean Cruise.

BILL GLAZER

e or strategy exposed to you at **The American Retail Supply,**
on **Conference & Expo** by one of the speakers or one of the
your income in 2007?

HURRY! YOUR

OPPORTUNITY TO

REGISTER FOR THIS

FREE EVENT EXPIRES

ON AUGUST 21, 2006.

Looking forward to seeing

you in Seattle,

Bill Glazer

st of everyone who is already registered to attend what is turning into the
BUILDING Event ever put together for Independent Retailers and I was
gistered. Seriously, what the devil are you thinking?

ting, procrastinating is going to lock you out. We're

nearly 85% sold out.

ations come in. **IF YOU MESS AROUND MUCH LONGER YOU**
s nothing I can do to make more room. (The Convention Center has very
I not allow one person over their allowable number.)

rations between now and the end of the month because all of the speakers
eir own lists.

ng to GUARANTEE the extraordinary value
U of this FREE Conference & Expo
I will put $100.00 of my own money right on the line

with my...

PERSONAL, MAKE-YOU-HAPPY GUARANTEE
THAT THIS WILL BE THE MOST VALUABLE EVENT
EVER HAVING TO DO WITH MAKING REALLY BIG MONEY
IN THE RETAIL INDUSTRY

I want you to register for this FREE event (my gift to you) without an ounce of concern over how much it
will be worth to you. Even though the seminar is FREE, you'll still have to cover your airfare, hotel and
food, so I want you to have an ironclad, unwavering confidence that you are making a wise decision for
yourself and/or your family. So, I'm going to go way, way, out on a limb for you:

Attend BOTH days, in their entirety, and if you honestly feel I have
overstated the value of this event, under-delivered on my promises,

You can see this in full color when you claim your FREE CD
of all of the exhibits in this book by using the form on page 312.

121

First, you see the puzzle piece and the words "I'm puzzled," and soon you learn that the puzzle piece can win you a cruise. After looking closely at the puzzle piece, your eyes scan the page and you see a paper-clipped handwritten note from me urging you to hurry. This is not only a double readership path, but actually a form of double testimonial by adding my voice into the sales letter.

This is a great example of how the double readership path is perfectly utilized for longer copy. In this case, the sales letter was sixteen pages. As you scan Keith's sales letter, notice the elements of this letter that catch your eyes. You see the puzzle piece, the paper-clipped handwritten note, bold words, larger font, different fonts, shaded boxes, photos, etc., and the more you see, the deeper you want to read.

rubber band mailer

Dr. Greg Nielsen, mentioned more than once in this book, is a brilliant marketer who knows how to translate a simple idea that everyone knows about into a brilliant marketing technique.

And everyone knows that you put a rubber band around your wrist to remind yourself of something. Well, Dr. Nielsen thought it would be good if he helped his customers remind themselves that they may have unused health benefits expiring soon.

STAFF MEMO

How To Use Your "Flex-Plan" To Give Yourself The Best Christmas Gift Ever!

If You're A Busy Woman, Then You Have To Hurry And Use Your Group Insurance Flex-Plan Before The End Of This Year!

FROM: Dr. Nielsen's Staff
    (just Marie this time)
    505 Aber Drive
    Waterford, WI 53185-0086
    Phone: (262) 534-3767

Monday, 2:33 PM

Dear Friend:

Happy Holidays!

It's me (Marie) from Dr. Nielsen's office. As you can see, I've enclosed a big "hot pink" rubber band with this letter. So, why did I do this, you ask? Well, there are <u>two</u> really important reasons:

1) *I have something **URGENT** to tell you and I wanted to make certain I got your undivided attention ...and...*

2) *Since you may have <u>unused</u> health insurance benefits that are about to expire at the end of this year, I decided to enclose a rubber band that you can wear on your wrist to remind you to use these benefits up!*

Anyway, I was checking our records today and I noticed that many patients still have unused health benefits that expire at the end of this year. After December 31st, they can never be used again. Oh man, if you have

(please go to the next page)

-Page 1-

You can see this in full color when you claim your FREE CD of all of the exhibits in this book by using the form on page 312.

Clearly this is a great example of the double readership path. The rubber band is taped to the first page of the letter along with all of the graphic enhancements (headline, test in a box, bolding, lists, subheads, etc.) that are designed to grab your attention.

OUTRAGEOUS exercise

Give your sales letter to someone to read, having blacked out everything that is not featured cosmetically or graphically, and then see if he or she can get the complete concept of what you are offering. If he or she can, you've achieved the double readership path.

Although Dr. Nielsen did not use personalization in his sales letter, he did do something very interesting. Actually it was OUTRAGEOUSLY interesting.

Instead of Dr. Nielsen himself sending out the letter, he sent it out as a staff memo. It comes from Doctor Nielsen's staff, but wait, look closer— "(just Marie this time)" is in the return address.

Wow. Most likely, his patients know Marie, and so it's been personalized. Marie sent this. This is a great example of an inexpensive form of personalization.

Graphically, obviously, the rubber band and layout of the "staff memo" bring a lot of attention. And the copy—this personal letter from Marie—is conversational and helpful, and it gives a great reason why the rubber band is there.

OUTRAGEOUS boost

Items that are attached to your sales messages such as a nickel, a puzzle piece, and a rubber band are called GRABBERS because they "grab" the recipients' attention. Grabbers are another tool to increase response and should be used as often as possible. As you can see, they don't need to be fancy or expensive. Heck, you can't get much less expensive than taping a rubber band to a piece of paper! For more details about grabbers, see chapter 13.

photos & illustrations

Dress up in a straitjacket and make some crazy money? Sure, sign me up.

I did exactly that. Then I created a great headline that included a reason why I was in the straitjacket. I added some crazy graphics onto an oversized postcard and mailed it out.

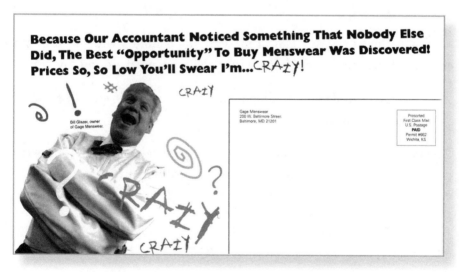

You can see this in full color when you claim your FREE CD of all of the exhibits in this book by using the form on page 312.

Crazy? You betcha! It was crazy fun watching the customers roll through the doors at my stores.

Now I want you to do something. Take a look at the crazy straitjacket postcard and imagine it without the photo of me in the straitjacket.

Is it still effective?

Maybe ... but it is definitely not <u>AS</u> effective!

The photo of me really helps to relay the story much better than if the photo was not there. That is exactly how to use photos to your advantage in your OUTRAGEOUS advertising.

You want them to enhance your stories. Remember the old saying that a picture can tell a thousand words. Well, I'm not sure they can tell a thousand words, but they sure can deliver a much clearer message.

I love using pictures in my advertising. It's not beneath me to portray myself in a way that will make customers and prospects notice. Instead, it's fun.

bill behind bars

Once I had a photo taken of me standing behind a wrought iron fence holding a black mug in my hand with a chain wrapped around my wrists.

This was a simple way to snap a picture that made it look like I was in, of all places ... prison!!!

I used this photo in one of the most successful ads I ever ran for my retail stores, and I took quite a bit of good-natured ribbing from my customers at the same time (as you'd expect).

First, let's look at the envelope that the OUTRAGEOUS advertisement went out in.

You can see this in full color when you claim your FREE CD of all of the exhibits in this book by using the form on page 312.

The few words on that envelope are enough to make you want to look inside because it makes you wonder what people are calling "illegal." And then you open the envelope, and on the first page of a flyer (on next page), you see me behind bars.

There I am, coffee cup in hand, banging on the bars because I am imprisoned for selling at:

"PRICES SO LOW... YOU'LL SWEAR THIS IS ILLEGAL"

Once again, this is a great example of how you can have a lot of fun and make a strong point at the same time.

Quickly, a comparison is made as if on a large-font quiz, and the checkmark is placed in the proper box—the box that says, "Shop at Gage and save some <u>REAL MONEY</u>."

You can see this in full color when you claim your FREE CD of all of the exhibits in this book by using the form on page 312.

And then it becomes a letter to a preferred customer and friend explaining (using double readership path) that this is the "<u>MOST GENEROUS OFFER WE HAVE EVER MADE</u>."

It goes on to describe the offer and then use humorous memorable language calling my coupons "ethical bribes." Finally, this page has a hand-drawn arrow pointing the reader to look inside for more.

Once the sales letter is opened, fourteen photos of merchandise appear with a description of each. And under it all is a question-and-answer section explaining the sale.

Finally, one more feature of this page is the handwriting, which is used to emphasize, in a personal way, what needs to be pointed out—such as the name brands.

And then the final page comes back to the ethical bribes. It offers a recap list and four final points to remember.

The entire letter is filled with information for all kinds of readers. There are graphics—even funny graphics of me behind bars—that originally catch your attention in an OUTRAGEOUS way, and then I show the offer in a way that backs up my OUTRAGEOUS claim.

OUTRAGEOUS boost

When using photos, try to place captions beneath them in order to further enhance your story. People have been trained by newspapers and magazines to read captions beneath photos. In fact, in those media it is the second most read part of an article (second to the headline). As you can see beneath the photo of me behind bars, I wrote a caption that read, **"BILL GLAZER BEHIND BARS: Gage Menswear Owner is mistakenly jailed. Local authorities suspected Gage's low prices hinted towards illegal activity by the 56-year-old store."**

---

illustrations – no b.s.

Photos aren't the only way to portray a story.

You can also use illustrations just as effectively. For example, Dan Kennedy, my business partner at Glazer-Kennedy Insider's Circle, is famous for his no B.S. approach as well as for writing the monthly No B.S. Marketing Letter— (which is the number-one most read marketing newsletter on the planet).

An illustration, a cartoon character of Dan sitting on top of a bull, with a caption beneath it is often shown in the newsletter. A real photo of Dan sitting on top of a bull has also been used, but results actually have shown that in this case, the cartoon Dan wins out.

Dan Kennedy's famous cartoon sitting on top of a bull,
illustrating the no B.S. approach that he's famous for.

OUTRAGEOUS resource

You can take a FREE test-drive of two full months of Dan Kennedy's No B.S. Letter and "ELITE" Gold Membership at www.dankennedy.com.

copydoodles

One of my best secrets for increasing response to all of my OUTRAGEOUS advertising is a simple-to-use software program that you install on your computer called CopyDoodles.

You've probably noticed several times in the examples that I've been showing you handwritten graphics and fonts that make the copy look much more interesting.

Mike Capuzzi, a member of one of my VIP Coaching Groups, realized that these little interesting additions to his advertisements substantially increased response, so he created hundreds and hundreds for his own use.

When others saw them, they literally begged him to make them available, and he created an easy-to-use tool as the ultimate shortcut.

In fact, I rarely write anything anymore where I don't use them. This includes:

- sales letters
- Web sites
- e-mails
- postcards
- memos
- faxes
- signs

In fact, everywhere I use words to sell something.

OUTRAGEOUS resource

Information about CopyDoodles can be found at www. copyenhancements.com.

Just to prove it to you, let me show you some actual examples of how CopyDoodles increased response.

web site test

Before

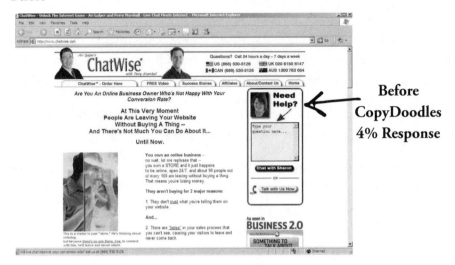

Before
CopyDoodles
4% Response

After

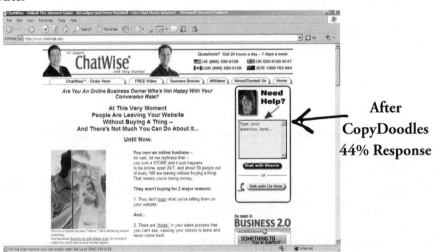

After
CopyDoodles
44% Response

sales letter test

Before

← **Before CopyDoodles 2.5% Response**

After

← **After CopyDoodles 13.8% Response**

envelope test

Before

Before
CopyDoodles
1.1% Response

After

After
CopyDoodles
8.7% Response

order form test

Before

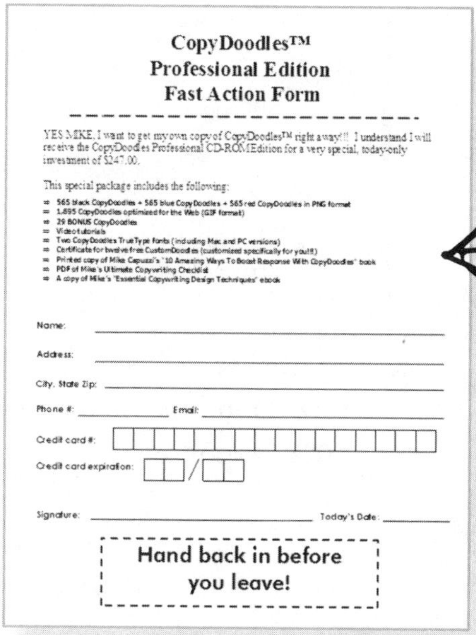

CopyDoodles™
Professional Edition
Fast Action Form

YES MIKE, I want to get my own copy of CopyDoodles™ right away!!! I understand I will receive the CopyDoodles Professional CD-ROM Edition for a very special, today-only investment of $247.00.

This special package includes the following:

- 565 black CopyDoodles + 565 blue CopyDoodles + 565 red CopyDoodles in PNG format
- 1,695 CopyDoodles optimized for the Web (GIF format)
- 29 BONUS CopyDoodles
- Video tutorials
- Two CopyDoodles TrueType fonts (including Mac and PC versions)
- Certificate for twelve free CustomDoodles (customized specifically for you!!)
- Printed copy of Mike Capuzzi's "10 Amazing Ways To Boost Response With CopyDoodles" book
- PDF of Mike's Ultimate Copywriting Checklist
- A copy of Mike's "Essential Copywriting Design Techniques" ebook

Name:
Address:
City, State Zip:
Phone #: Email:
Credit card #:
Credit card expiration: /
Signature: Today's Date:

Hand back in before you leave!

Before CopyDoodles 13.8% Response

After

CopyDoodles™
Professional Edition
Fast Action Form

YES Mike, I want to get my own copy of CopyDoodles™ right away!!! I understand I will receive the CopyDoodles Professional CD-ROM Edition for a very special investment of Today only $247

This package includes all of the following on one CD-ROM:

- 565 black CopyDoodles + 565 blue CopyDoodles + 565 red CopyDoodles in PNG format
- 1,695 CopyDoodles optimized for the Web (GIF format)
- 29 BONUS CopyDoodles
- Video tutorials
- Two CopyDoodles TrueType fonts (including Mac and PC versions)
- Certificate for twelve free CustomDoodles (customized specifically for you!!)
- Printed copy of Mike Capuzzi's "10 Amazing Ways To Boost Response With CopyDoodles" book
- PDF of Mike's Ultimate Copywriting Checklist
- A copy of Mike's "Essential Copywriting Design Techniques" ebook

Name:
Address:
City, State Zip:
Phone #: Email:
Credit card #:
Credit card expiration: /
Signature: Today's Date:

Hand back in before you leave!

VALID TODAY ONLY

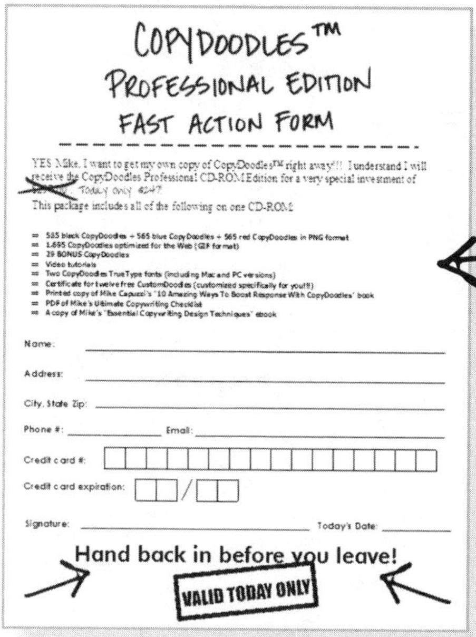

After CopyDoodles 33.1% Response

postcard test

Before

**Before
CopyDoodles
0.0% Response**

After

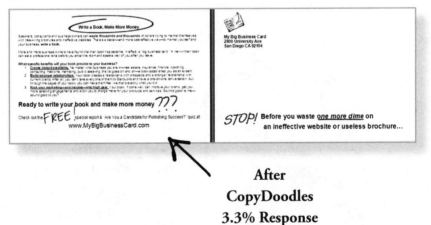

**After
CopyDoodles
3.3% Response**

S.O.S.

Sizzling Outrageous Summation

1) Extra elements bring extra profits.

2) Everybody likes to see their name.

3) People look at advertisements by using the double readership path.

4) Pictures and illustrations can really help to tell your story.

5) Making your copy interesting increases readership.

6) CopyDoodles bring oodles of responses.

7) Harnessing The Power Of Testimonials

How do you make a decision on where to eat on Friday night?

Do you open the yellow pages and look for a restaurant, call them, and ask if they would recommend a restaurant for tonight? Of course not! They would recommend their own restaurant.

Instead, you call a friend.

You call a friend or you consult a review or you read a guidebook. Why is that? Because **what people say about you is "at least" ten times more believable than what you say about yourself.**

If an outside source with a real name recommends something to you, you tend to believe it because you inherently expect this person to tell you the truth. He or she doesn't have a material interest in your decision to purchase. This person is simply telling you what he or she likes through his or her own experiences. And that's powerful. OUTRAGEOUSLY powerful!!

why you need testimonials

Unfortunately, most people won't believe you when you are selling something, because you are the one who is going to profit from the sale. And few people have the confidence in their own ability to make a good decision. And so, getting someone else to recommend you helps … a lot.

The easiest and most efficient way to get others to recommend you in your OUTRAGEOUS advertising is to use testimonials.

What is a testimonial?

Webster's Dictionary defines testimonial as "a written or said recommendation or as an expression of esteem or appreciation."

While this is true, some testimonials are better than others. These are what I call "good" testimonials.

A good testimonial does one of two things:

    1) It relays a "specific" outcome

        OR

    2) It overcomes an objective

Both kinds of testimonials are important to include.

A good outcome is relayed by someone who has been a customer of yours, is believable, and is helpful. This is a place where I see a lot of entrepreneurs make a mistake.

For example, you'll often see what people think are outcome testimonials where they say they saved hundreds of dollars or were happy with the product or service for whatever reason. While these words are helpful, they are too general and are not very powerful.

A "specific" outcome testimonial relays a specific outcome.

For example, instead of saying, "I saved hundreds of dollars," a good outcome testimonial would say, "I saved $213.92."

Or, instead of saying, "I was happy with your product or service," a good outcome testimonial would say, "When I used your audio course to teach me how to speak Japanese, I was amazed that I could master the language in just nine short weeks."

Hopefully you see the subtle but powerful difference between a generic outcome testimonial and a specific outcome testimonial. Obviously, the specific ones are much more believable, and that's what you are attempting to achieve ... people believing they are true.

And it's the same when a customer of yours gives a testimonial that overcomes an objection.

These types of testimonials are just as powerful as outcome testimonials because when you bring up and overcome objections, it significantly helps your sales process.

Let me give you an example. Let's say you are providing a weight loss product and you find out that many of your customers procrastinate before they engage your services.

A great example of a testimonial to overcome procrastination would sound something like this:

"I can't believe I waited an entire year before I became a customer of the Take It Off Fast Centers. I could have been 20 pounds lighter 12 months ago and felt great about putting on my swimsuit while I was vacationing in the Bahamas last year."

Can you see how these types of testimonials can get people to take action? It's important that you figure out every reason why someone might not buy and have a customer testimonial to overcome each.

OUTRAGEOUS exercise

Develop a list of all of the reasons why someone might not buy your products or services. Make the list as long as you can because the longer the list, the better the chance you'll be able to overcome every objection that someone might have.

A great place to get help with developing a very complete list is to ask your prospects/customers/clients/patients what their objections were before they bought.

how to get testimonials

I've been in business a long time, and after many years of expecting (and hoping) that people would "automatically" give me great testimonials, I discovered that there is one best way to get them.

The best way to get testimonials is to … simply ask for them—and then make it easy for the customer to give them.

I know this might sound a bit obvious, but that's how you get them. People don't often volunteer praise that you can use publicly, but when you ask for it, praise is surprisingly easy to acquire as long as you've earned it.

But, as in much of life, a key to getting good testimonials is timing. So what you want to do is look at the entire experience that a customer has when he or she does business with you and figure out what is the "best" time to ask for testimonials.

For example, in my retail stores we discovered that the best time to ask for a testimonial is when the transaction is finished and the customer or client says, "Thank you." That's the sweet spot.

At that moment, you essentially have the customer's full permission to turn to him or her—and you have to train yourself and your staff to do this—and ask, "Can you do me a favor?"

This is what we discovered. When someone thanks you for your service and product, he or she is actually thanking you for your expertise and therefore will always say "YES" when asked to do you a favor.

After he or she says yes, we always respond with, "I really appreciate your thanks, but would you take just a few seconds and write down for me why you enjoyed doing business with us so I can show it to others I can help just like you?"

And have a sheet of paper sitting there already prepared for the customer to write down his or her thoughts.

Another example is what we developed with a client of mine who sold new windows for homeowners. There we set up the testimonial at the beginning of the selling process.

In this case, we told clients that we were going to do a great job when we installed their new windows and all we asked in return was that after we installed them and proved we'd done a great job, the clients would put in writing the experience that they had dealing with the window replacement company.

Once again, it's all timing, and you have to determine when is the best time when you are dealing with your customers/clients/patients to "ask" for testimonials.

OUTRAGEOUS exercise

Write down every "step" that your customers/clients/ patients experience when they do business with you and decide which step is the best time to ask them to give you a testimonial about their experience with you or your company. NOTE: You might find that you have to test a few steps before you find out which one is best.

Of course you can help to prep them with their testimonials. Let's go back to our weight loss example from above. If you have clients who told you they procrastinated before they purchased your weight loss service, you could say to them that you'd really appreciate them writing about how waiting a year turned out to be a big mistake.

Remember, when asking for testimonials, you always want them to address one of the two purposes ...

1) Relays a "specific" outcome

2) Overcomes an objective

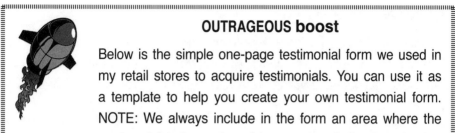

OUTRAGEOUS boost

Below is the simple one-page testimonial form we used in my retail stores to acquire testimonials. You can use it as a template to help you create your own testimonial form. NOTE: We always include in the form an area where the person giving the testimonial grants permission for using it.

Testimonial Form

Name:_____

Address:_____

City _____ State _____ Zip _____

Occupation:_____

Number of years as our client: _____

What is your overall feeling about (store name)?

_____

_____

Describe in detail what part of your shopping experience made you the happiest:

_____

_____

Describe the one or two most important benefits you've gotten the most from shopping with us... Please explain specifically what you've gained from the experience:

_____

_____

_____

Thank you... We really appreciate your honest answers.

____ I do not mind if you use my name and comments in any or all of your promotional materials.

Signature: _____

Date: _____

people are skeptical

It's a well-known fact that people are skeptical about testimonials. They often see them but don't believe they're real. For example, if they see a testimonial that's signed with just initials, often they think it's made up.

So what you want to do is make sure that as much information as possible is given about the person who is giving the testimonial. The more information you can include about the person giving the testimonial, the better.

At my menswear store, we ALWAYS included their full name, and we liked to include their occupation, how many years they'd been a customer, and their hometown in any testimonial we offered. We wanted others to know that they could believe our customers—because they are "real," not made-up people.

OUTRAGEOUS boost

The information gathered to use for testimonials has the extra benefit of being added to your customer database, and people who give you testimonials often become your best repeat customers.

how to present testimonials

OUTRAGEOUS boost

Blank space in your OUTRAGEOUS advertising doesn't sell anything. If there is blank space, put a testimonial there and let that previously blank space now go to work for you to make your product or service more believable.

Although there are lots of ways to effectively present testimonials, simply presenting them at all is effective because once again (it's worth repeating)

what other people say about you is ten times more effective than anything you can say yourself. So use them!

Use as many as you can use, and use them wherever you can use them. However, presenting them so that they stand out can be done in a number of ways. Some of my favorite ways to get them to stand out are:

- Use a different font for each testimonial.
- Highlight or capitalize some of the key words in the testimonial.
- Use a different color ink.
- Put a box around them.
- Show a photo of the person giving the testimonial.
- Place a headline above the testimonial that encourages someone to read it.

Again, I emphasize that you want to give the customer a chance to hear other people say things about you that are ten times as effective as anything you could say about yourself.

Finally, they can be long or they can be short. I've used four-page testimonials. I've used two sentences. It depends on the situation. Devoid of an opportunity to present a long testimonial letter (if you can), it is best to load up an ad with as many short testimonials as possible.

in all media

If you have testimonials, you can use them more than once.

You can use a testimonial, for instance, in a direct mail piece, a Web advertisement, a magazine ad, and, if you got the person to record it, for radio or television or a Webinar.

One of my favorite ways to use testimonials was done at my own menswear stores: whenever we put someone "on hold," we had him or her listen to a six-minute continuous recording of our customers' testimonials about how they liked shopping with us and some of the great services we provided.

As a matter of fact, you should always attempt to put testimonials in all of your OUTRAGEOUS advertising. I have never seen a case where a properly written and placed testimonial did any harm. They are a great benefit!

testimonials in action

Here are some examples of the use of testimonials in OUTRAGEOUS advertising.

This section will focus on the use of testimonials, but there are other aspects of OUTRAGEOUS advertising to point out as well.

The coin mailer

This example comes from England. That's why the coin you see in the corner is an English tuppence.

Jon McCulloch is a freelance copywriter and certainly understands the power of testimonials, so he uses them to attract more clients for himself.

As you can see, he used the coin as a grabber to grab your attention, and then he goes on to talk in first person using some very good copy to reach the customer.

Page 1 of Jon McCulloch's COIN MAILER. You can see this in full color when you claim your FREE CD of all of the exhibits in this book by using the form on page 312.

But then when you flip the page over, you see the back is loaded with twelve testimonials of "Success Stories From People Jon Is Making Rich." Take a look.

> ## "Success Stories From People Jon Is Making <u>RICH</u>!"
>
> I run my marketing like a military operation - I've no time for excuses or second best. Results are all that matter. So discovering nonconformist British copywriter Jon McCulloch was like taking a faceful of smelling salts. It's sharp, perceptive, and works fast... and his copy leaps out of the page and hits you right between the eyes. It's like James Bond with a typewriter. Listen - Jon's aiming for the top, right up there with the "Big Names". So get him on your side NOW before he figures out he should be charging big, big money."
> **Scott Tucker, Winner Glazer-Kennedy Inner-Circle Marketer of the Year 2006.**
> www.MortgageMarketingGenius.com, www.fromdebttosavings.com
>
> "We very recently had a client dump on us and it was real 'balls to the wall' time. I called Jon and he gave me one strategy - JUST ONE - that I used the VERY NEXT DAY to get us right out of the hole and back on our feet again. I can't possibly thank Jon enough. He literally saved my business - in ONE phone call. He is brilliant. Seriously: if YOU have a problem with your marketing you MUST speak to Jon. He can solve it. Period."
> **Henry Bond, Anglian Events**
> www.anglianevents.co.uk, www.tellhenry.com
>
> "Jon is a natural born copywriter, and the only guy I turn to when I want copy that truly sells. I've used a number of "celebrity copywriters", and each time I have been charged an arm-and-a-leg for copy that couldn't even beat my own controls, and I am not even a copywriter! Finding Jon was like finding bags of gold under my bed. Here's a guy who not only has his 'own voice', something truly rare in the field of copywriting, but also guarantees his work will outperform any of your existing controls... or you don't pay him. I just couldn't resist, and Jon's work has proven itself right where it matters... in my bank balance!"
> **Rob Taylor, Megastep International,**
> www.megastep.com
>
> "If you want maximum return on your marketing investment then the sales message has to be ABSOLUTELY top notch. When you get Jon to write your sales messages it's like owning the rights to LEGALLY print money!"
> **Joe Gregory, co-author, "The Gorillas Want Bananas: The Lean Marketing Bible for Expert Businesses", www.gorillaswantbananas.com**
>
> "When I first started to work with Jon McCulloch, I was initially sceptical. But his enthusiasm and drive are infectious and his ideas are way 'out there', completely maverick and sometimes just plain weird. Within literally *just two days* of taking his advice, I started to see an immediate improvement in my business and the way I handled it. He has changed completely how I see and run my business. I think Jon is a marketing genius. Using his materials and implementing just some of his ideas I have increased my profits by over 50% within just 6 months and end up working less to make them. My only question to Jon is 'how can I give you more money so you can make them even bigger?'"
> **Ant Watt, Health Muscle and Fitness, Ipswich,**
> www.heroesmuscle.co.uk
>
> "We've been using Jon as our copywriter for a couple of years now and he never fails to deliver strong, bold, and persuasive copy on time every time. He writes in a powerful and compelling conversational tone that hits home right where we want it to – and gets us exactly the results we need. We recently carried out a mailing campaign to our current client list which resulted on first mailing in a response rate of 15%. A rule of thumb for any business is "use the best copywriter you can afford". I'd second this – using Jon is an investment of our time and money that pays off manyfold."
> **Hayley Aylott, Financial Planning Matters**
>
> "I know just by looking instantly, when Jon has had his hands on a project – the quality just shines through. Jon's reputation is utterly deserved: he really is the best in the business."
> **Mary Gregory, Fabulous Functions Ltd**
>
> "Jon has worked extensively on our website and advertising copy, and has even rewritten our Quality Statement. We've always found his services to be first class – he consistently gave us great copy with a very short turnaround time. He's friendly, approachable and forthright and he maintains a positive and professional approach to his work that makes working with him a pleasure. We'd definitely recommend Jon to anyone thinking of using a freelance copywriter."
> **Robert Gordon, Director of Business Development, Riskaware Limited**
> www.riskaware.co.uk
>
> "Jon is an excellent copywriter, delivering great copy quickly and efficiently. And to top it all, he works with such enthusiasm and professionalism, I can't imagine using anyone else."
> **Matt Porter, Matt Porter Web Design.**
> www.mattporter.com
>
> "By using the appropriate language Jon has enabled us to express that ours is a preferential business attracting calibre customers and thereby increasing the number of quality enquiries we receive. His business has greatly benefited our business; his professionalism has freed us to work in our own field of professionalism. We recommend his services highly to anyone in business who is undertaking any form of advertising or marketing"
> **Theresa Barnes, TB Interiors, Cambridge**
> www.tbinteriors.co.uk
>
> "...we received the first draft, which was perfect. It was short, concise, punchy and delivered our message in exactly the right way. We would not hesitate to recommend Jon's services to others."
> **Lisa Andrews, Business Development Manager, KeConnect Internet,**
> www.keconnect.co.uk
>
> "Jon delivered a set of drafts that not only encapsulated everything about me and my business but did so in a fresh, engaging, and compelling way. Not only that, but he has since made changes and offered advice, all free of charge. Jon really went the extra distance to give me terrific copy and fantastic value for money. If you need any kind of copy, whether for sales and marketing materials or your website, I strongly recommend you to Jon McCulloch before you speak to anyone else."
> **Peter Heath, Living Pilates,**
> www.livingpilates.co.uk

Page 2 of Jon McCulloh's COIN MAILER. You can see this in full color when you claim your FREE CD of all of the exhibits in this book by using the form on page 312.

Jon placed twelve one-paragraph or so testimonials from satisfied clients on the back of his OUTRAGEOUS letter because he knows that what people say about you is ten times as effective as anything you could say about yourself.

He further added credibility to each of the testimonials by giving their full names, business names, and Web sites.

Carefully read each of the testimonials and pay close attention to how he mixes outcome and objection-overcoming testimonials.

Accu-Tax advertisement in a Community Supplement Newspaper

"Our appointment book has been three times as busy as last year."

That's a testimonial that Gary Shapiro of Bullhead City, Arizona, wrote to me about some help I gave him in his advertising. Gary actually wrote me a two-page letter that I use in my advertising, but I want to point out how he uses testimonials in his successful OUTRAGEOUS advertising.

Accu-Tax's NEWSPAPER AD. You can see this in full color when you claim your FREE CD of all of the exhibits in this book by using the form on page 312.

Of course, your eyes immediately go to the heart in the middle of the advertisement. "WE LOVE SOLVING IRS PROBLEMS!" But as you see that and realize what this is about, you also notice, right outside the heart, the words of satisfied customers.

And if you look closely, you will see that only a first initial and last name is used. Although you do want to use full names whenever you can, sometimes, as in the area of tax returns, customers are more comfortable only putting part of their name where confidential information is talked about.

The rest of the advertisement includes all the essential elements: a headline, an offer, and a deadline—one time only. But the adding of the extra element of testimonials resulted in helping them to triple their appointments from the previous year ... THAT'S THE POWER OF TESTIMONIALS.

gage 56th anniversary sale

Don't take our word for it, take a look at what our clients say about us ...

In this particular advertisement from my menswear store, we were sending out gift certificates for discounts off of our merchandise because of our anniversary. I put a headline on it and personalized it by writing it from me to you, and there was a deadline printed on the OUTRAGEOUS coupons. But there was more when you flipped it over.

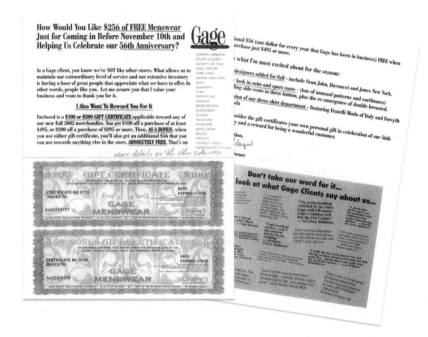

FRONT AND BACK OF GAGE ANNIVERSARY AD. *You can see this in full color when you claim your FREE CD of all of the exhibits in this book by using the form on page 312.*

When the customer gets to the back of the letter, there is a clear section at the bottom of the page stating:

Don't take our word for it...
Take a look at what Gage clients say about us...

The important thing here is the use of the quotes and the font that is used. Each testimonial is in a different font, making it appear as if each was actually copied from the original letter. Again, just a little extra OUTRAGEOUS touch that increases the odds of the copy being read.

OUTRAGEOUS resource

Your business should conduct an anniversary sale or event every year because an anniversary is a credible reason for conducting something special. In fact, I've seen many survey results that prove this. Of course milestone anniversaries, such as 5, 10, 20, 25, and 50 years, should be handled as even more special because people really love to participate in them. I teach this strategy in great detail in my Platinum Business Building Marketing System, available at bgsmarketing.com.

free wallet coupon in the gage nickel mailer

In chapter 6, I described a campaign during which I sent out a nickel in the mail to promote a Buy-1-Get-1-for-5¢ sale.

There was one more element to that campaign—a premium (see chapter 8 for more on premiums) of a free wallet with any purchase during the sale. I enclosed a coupon.

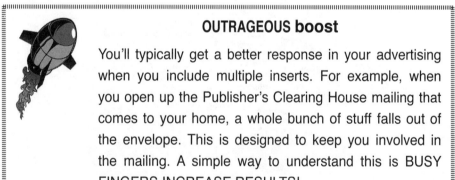

We Couldn't Have Said it Better Ourselves.

 Gage Menswear provides good quality and excellent service. I know the salespeople are attentive and honest by the compliments I get on my clothing.
~ Steven Friedman, Reisterstown, MD

 Gage is my "gauge" for success! Finally, I've found an attentive, friendly menswear store. You have an excellent quality of clothing!
~ Mary Cary, Baltimore, MD

The salespeople at Gage World Class Menswear are awesome! And, Gage carries sizes that fit me well! I've been shopping at Gage for over 37 years!
~ Van Williams, Baltimore, MD

I've been a Gage World Class Menswear client for 30 years now and I have to tell you....I have always been able to get the best quality clothing at the absolutely best prices from day one! Being able to find such well-made clothing is a rarity in today's marketplace.
~ Jerry Anderson, Baltimore, MD

 Gage Menswear makes shopping for all my boys an easy, enjoyable experience! We receive just the right amount of help in finding the correct fitting suit. With 5 boys still at home, I'm always looking for the nicest suits at the best prices.
~ Chana Price, Baltimore, MD

 After 15 years of shopping here, I "Gage" the competition based on the knowledge of your sales staff. Gage offers good quality, good service and doesn't try to sell more than the client needs.
~ Larry Goldberg, Baltimore, MD

FRONT AND BACK of Gage's FREE wallet coupon. You can see this in full color when you claim your FREE CD of all of the exhibits in this book by using the form on page 312.

When I first looked at the proof of the coupon, I noticed that the back of it was blank. As I've mentioned before, blank space won't sell anything and is a waste. So I filled it up with six great testimonials—a much better use of space.

OUTRAGEOUS boost

You'll typically get a better response in your advertising when you include multiple inserts. For example, when you open up the Publisher's Clearing House mailing that comes to your home, a whole bunch of stuff falls out of the envelope. This is designed to keep you involved in the mailing. A simple way to understand this is BUSY FINGERS INCREASE RESULTS!

---

scott tucker's "babe" tear sheet mailing

Scott Tucker is a former loan officer who now teaches other loan officers how to grow their businesses. This happens often when you get good at OUTRAGEOUS advertising. You exit your everyday job and start teaching others how to do what you've mastered. In fact, that's exactly what happened to me. I became so good at marketing and advertising in my retail business that I began teaching it to others.

Scott is an expert at creating what are commonly called "tear sheet" mailings. This is an advertisement that at first appears to be a newspaper or magazine article that's been ripped out and mailed to you. Typically it has a Post-it note attached to it with a handwritten note on it that says something like, "(Your First Name), Try This, It Works! J."

Tear sheet mailings are very effective when you learn how to write them and design them so they appear to be an actual newspaper or magazine story.

But Scott Tucker went an extra mile by making the following tear sheet mailing a long-form testimonial. It works on the tear sheet level and the testimonial level.

FRONT AND BACK of Scott Tucker's "Babe" tear sheet mailing.
You can see this in full size when you claim your FREE CD
of most of the exhibits in this book by using the form on page 312.

This is a great example of a long testimonial used to great advantage. And you'll notice that this very long-form testimonial tear sheet actually BOTH offers outcome and overcomes objections.

OUTRAGEOUS boost

The attractive girls in bathing suits on both sides of the tear sheet appear to be part of the adjacent article in the newspaper, but they are not. They are like a border, and these girls actually increase response by as much as 30 percent. You noticed them and so does everybody else—both men and women. They do the same thing that grabbers do on a sales letter.

NOTE: Don't be offended. I'm only teaching what works.

Sizzling Outrageous Summation

1) What someone says about you is "at least" ten times more believable than what you say about yourself.

2) The best testimonials either give a "specific" outcome or overcome an objection.

3) The best way to get testimonials is to ask for them at the right time.

4) Make it easy for people to give testimonials.

5) If you have blank space, fill it up with testimonials.

8) Using Premiums To Skyrocket Response

"Hey, just by walking into that store, they GAVE me one of these!"

When people get something for nothing (a premium—a free gift to entice the customer into the store), they love to brag about it. They tell everyone. And if they are offered a chance to get something for nothing just by being exposed to your merchandise, they'll often jump at the chance.

And then, while they're in your store, of course, while waiting to pick up the free gift, they often see something that they want to buy. Or maybe the gift is only given with a purchase.

Of course, stores are not the only place where premiums work. They work in just about any business. In addition to brick-and-mortar businesses, they work in direct mail; they work online; they work ... just about anywhere when properly deployed.

But here's the most important fact you need to understand about premiums: they typically increase response by "as much as" 30 percent, and in keeping with the OUTRAGEOUS message of this book ... they are fun to use.

the perceived value of premiums

When thinking about using premiums, you always want to keep in mind that a good premium has a much higher perceived value than its actual cost.

When offering a premium, you want to purchase them in bulk at a reasonable cost but present them to your customers at the retail price.

For instance, at my menswear store, we would often purchase items for less than five dollars and then we would give them away with a retail price value of as much as $30.

Perceived value has real value, both to your customers and to you. By simply declaring that you are giving away a valuable gift, it brings more interest. Of course, you still have to give away something decent.

OUTRAGEOUS resource

Here are a couple of great places to find great quality premiums:

Insert information for:

* ASD/AMD: www.asdamd.com.

* 3D Mailer: www.outrageous-advertising.com/3DMailings/.

---

the free $20 umbrella

By now, you may have noticed that all of these advertising concepts fit together. And that's especially true of premiums—it is an important component part of a bigger campaign.

For instance, at my menswear store, I gave premiums away, including a drip-free umbrella. But before I get to the premium, I'd like to quickly point out that it was sent in a very important-looking self-mailer … A WESTERN UNION MAILGRAM.

The reason I chose this format was to get my mailing into the A pile. After all, when you think about receiving something from Western Union, what do you think?

Most people are thinking that this has something to do with money. For years, Western Union telegrams were used to notify people that someone recently passed away and they were named in that person's will. Western Union and money matters go hand in hand.

Western Union Mailgram. You can see this in full color when you claim your FREE CD of all of the exhibits in this book by using the form on page 312 .

And so as you can see, this letter was sent by an actual Western Union Mailgram, and in it I am announcing a new four-day sale (a good deadline, see chapter 5) and offering two free gifts—free parking at the lot next door and an umbrella that I make sure is clear to see in a coupon highlighted by one word:

FREE

OUTRAGEOUS boost

Free is one of the two most powerful words in advertising (the other being new).

And then you read that you are getting a $20 umbrella. Plus, when you look deeper into the letter, you will see that I say, "This is arguably the best umbrella you will ever own."

And it was a really wonderful umbrella, an actual high-end mini umbrella. But here's a secret … I bought all these mini umbrellas for $2 apiece when the supplier decided to close them out. As you can imagine, if I said that, it wouldn't generate nearly the perceived value that I was able to generate just by … well, adding a zero to what I paid for them.

OUTRAGEOUS boost

Never overstate the retail value of the premium because it can challenge the credibility of your offer. For example, in the case of the umbrellas above, they actually did retail for $20. I just happened to find a resource that wanted to get rid of them, so I bought out his entire stock at an unheard-of price.

It's really cool how one extra zero can change the perceived value of something. And it's so simple to do.

And here's the best part: it increased our response by 32 percent!

the "your-choice" premium

I offered a lot of different premiums in my menswear stores, and I did it in many different ways. But one thing I learned is that not everyone likes everything. So, as I've suggested in other areas of OUTRAGEOUS advertising, consider giving your customers a choice of premiums.

For instance, when representatives of two different menswear manufacturers were coming to my store in association with a special money-savings event, I sent out an oversized postcard.

Gage Menswear's special event OVERSIZED POSTCARD. You can see this in full color when you claim your FREE CD of all of the exhibits in this book by using the form on page 312.

As you can see, this one-day event naming the manufacturers is part of the headline, but there is also a prominent offer for a premium—actually a "choice" of premiums.

FREE GIFT – YOUR CHOICE

And both are identified inside a big circle as a $25 value. The choice of a 35 mm camera or a traveling stationery set is an extra powerful way to use premiums. It appeals to different interests and customers, and yet anyone can recognize (because I pointed it out in a circle!) the value of either of these gifts.

OUTRAGEOUS **boost**

The best way to present a premium is to include three things:

(1) a photo of it

(2) a description of it including features and benefits

(3) the retail value

Let me give you another example of how you can (and should) give people a choice of which premium they want. Several years ago, I did some consulting for a bank that was looking to increase their market share in one of their branches.

When I interviewed them, they reported to me that once they got one of their customer service representatives "face-to-face" with a prospect it usually resulted in acquiring some business for the bank.

So, I developed a multi-step campaign using FREE premiums as the key marketing strategy. The first mailing was sent out in a bank deposit bag since I wanted to make sure that their mail got opened. After all, what better use of a bank deposit bag as an envelope than using it to actually promote a bank?

Farmers & Merchants' bank deposit bag. You can see this in full color when you claim your FREE CD of all of the exhibits in this book by using the form on page 312.

Of course a bank deposit bag will get opened in the BIG pile of mail because you've got to think that there's money inside of it!!!

Then I developed a three-page sales letter using the OUTRAGEOUSLY effective techniques taught in this book.

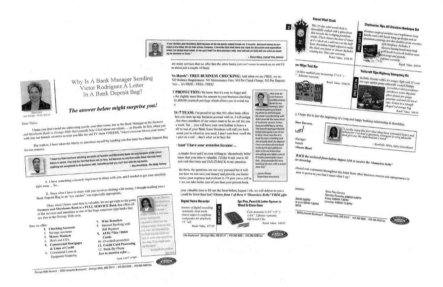

Farmers & Merchants' three-page new customer sales letter. You can see this in full color when you claim your FREE CD of all of the exhibits in this book by using the form on page 312.

And towards the bottom of page two and then continuing onto page three, you'll see I gave the prospects a choice of six different premiums. Since the customer value was so high at the bank, I was able to offer someone the choice of any one of the following:

1. electronic digital voice recorder

2. three-piece pen, pencil, and letter opener in a wood and glass case

3. Kassel wall clock

4. Chefmaster eighteen-piece all stainless-steel barbecue set

5. Maxam 101-piece tool set

6. Yorkcraft 15-piece highway emergency kit

As you can see, these aren't the typical cheap toasters that a bank offers to new customers, but we were able to buy these in small quantities from a supplier, so they only cost a fraction of the retail value.

OUTRAGEOUS boost

Giving a choice of premiums instead of just one is a very powerful marketing technique, which is called "INVOLVEMENT." In the case of the choice of premiums, you "involve" the prospect in thinking about which premium he wants versus whether he wants the premium at all. Typically involving the prospect will increase response even more.

connecting the premium to the OUTRAGEOUS campaign

Consistency is important in all aspects of OUTRAGEOUS advertising, and that includes the use of premiums.

Giving something away is great. Giving something away that somehow connects with the message you are relaying is important so that the recipient doesn't experience a disconnect. Let me give you an example of what I mean with the brown bag mailer.

brown bag mailer

Whenever I speak at a seminar on OUTRAGEOUS advertising, I always ask the audience how many of them have ever carried their lunch to school in a brown paper bag or have seen someone carry his or her lunch in a brown bag.

Of course, every hand in the room goes up.

So, everyone has seen a brown paper bag before, and they're familiar with its use. Of course, few have ever seen a brown paper bag in their mailbox, and it will solicit a similar response as the diner placemat mailing (as seen in chapter 4), which is, "What's this doing in my pile of mail?"

Of course this once again has to wind up in the recipient's A pile, which is exactly what you want!

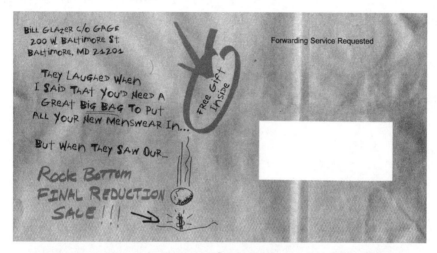

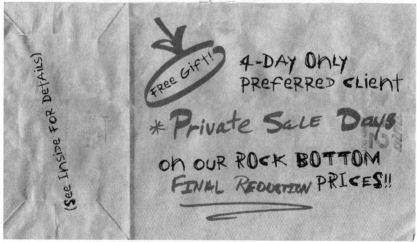

FRONT AND BACK of Gage Menswear's BROWN BAG mailing.
You can see this in full color when you claim your FREE CD
of all of the exhibits in this book by using the form on page 312.

And as you can see on the outside of the brown bag mailing, I intentionally draw attention to the absurdity of sending a brown bag in the mail by writing right on the envelope(er, outside of the bag):

"They laughed when I said you'd need a great big bag to put all your new Menswear in."

And so right away, you see it is a bag and I am making reference to a bag, plus I also not-so-subtly slip in the words "all your new Menswear."

But then, as you see, is the inside of the bag with writing all over it. It's a sea of information and precisely because it is written on a brown bag, you need to read more.

Gage Menswear's sales letter printed inside the BROWN BAG mailing.
You can see this in full color when you claim your FREE CD
of all of the exhibits in this book by using the form on page 312.

On here you find all sorts of information personalizing it (preferred client), giving a deadline (4-day only), and making an offer (73 percent off!!!). Plus there are many details about specific merchandise and the deadline is repeated, but then, at the bottom, is a hand-drawn coupon for a FREE BONUS of a zippered garment bag with a little sketch of the bag next to it.

So, this brown paper bag I sent in the mail to get attention includes a coupon for a garment bag that I am using to get attention. Synchronicity squared!

film processing mailer

You've got to give a reason why you are doing anything. That's how OUTRAGEOUS becomes OUTRAGEOUSLY believable.

So I came up with this great idea for sending out a pretend envelope for film processing and then explaining why I did it.

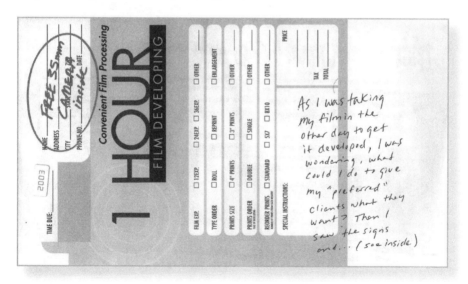

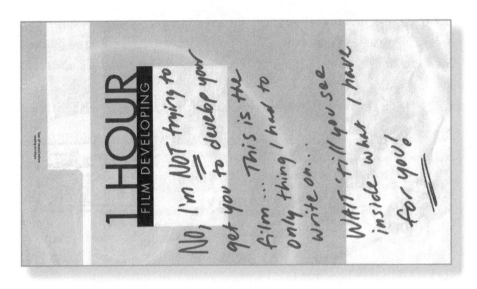

FRONT AND BACK of Gage Menswear's FILM DEVELOPING mailing.
You can see this in full color when you claim your FREE CD
of all of the exhibits in this book by using the form on page 312.

As you can see, I hint that I came up with the idea I am about to present as I was taking my film to get developed. I put this on the front of the film development envelope in handwriting. And that's the hint.

But there's one more thing on this envelope that you notice. It's an extra. It's a premium. It's a circled note up on the right-hand side that says:

"FREE 35 mm CAMERA inside"

So, unlike other regular mail, this OUTRAGEOUS piece demands that you look inside.

And inside, you find this.

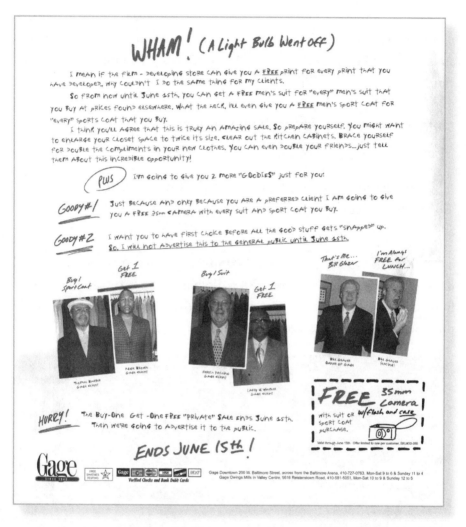

Gage Menswear's sales letter printed inside the FILM DEVELOPING mailing.
You can see this in full color when you claim your FREE CD
of all of the exhibits in this book by using the form on page 312.

I give an explanation of how I discovered a two-prints-for-one deal and thought that it would work for suits or for sport coats. And this offer of a premium has a different incentive-laden twist in that it is given WITH A PURCHASE!!!

171

On the coupon, "FREE" is in big letters and "with suit or sport coat purchase" is in smaller letters. That was for the customer's sake. In my mind, and in yours when you run such a sale fueled by a premium, the words "with a purchase" will be in bold.

premiums as part of more than one offer

When in doubt, pile it on.

That's the rule in so much of OUTRAGEOUS advertising, and it works as well with premiums as it does with everything else. OUTRAGEOUS advertising really does produce OUTRAGEOUS results.

And what's more OUTRAGEOUS than piling a premium on top of a discount for merchandise on top of a discount on gift certificates? I believe in the saying "the better the offer, the better the response." And I also believe that the better you tease, the more they read.

FRONT AND BACK of Gage Menswear's HOLIDAY POSTCARD mailing.
You can see this in full color when you claim your FREE CD
of all of the exhibits in this book by using the form on page 312.

By putting a silly image of myself on the card, I attracted attention, not to mention with a headline like:

Discover three MORE reasons why our competition hates us MORE THAN EVER this holiday!

That is a classic marketing headline that is sure to stir curiosity. Combined with my silly image, you are compelled to look inside. And just in case you are not, on the back is a circled reminder that a free gift offer is inside.

And inside is a repeat of the headline written on the postcard (headlines come in many different forms, see chapter 5) of three more reasons why our competition hates us.

3 more reasons why our competition hates us EVEN MORE at the holidays!

By now you are aware that Gage has the **LOWEST PRICES IN TOWN!** Over the last 90-days not one client has come forth finding better prices anywhere in town. That's great news, but the best news is that this Holiday season, even our lowest prices aren't low enough for you -- a V.I.P. client. That's right, you are one of our best clients and to thank you we want you to even **SAVE MORE**!

Take advantage of these extra savings before December 24th.

V.I.P. Bonus #1

The more you buy the more you save!

SAVE $10.⁰⁰, $20.⁰⁰, even $60.⁰⁰

SAVE

$10.00   On Any Purchase of $100.00 to $199.99 SKU#32-683

$20.00   On Any Purchase of $200.00 to $299.99 SKU#32-687

$60.00   On Any Purchase of $300.00 or More! SKU#32-686

May not be combined with past purchases or previous layaways. Expires 12/24/03.

V.I.P. Bonus #2

FREE
Pair of Designer Socks

With any purchase.

A $9.00 value. Limit one per client, while supplies last.
Expires 12/24/03.
SKU#32-684

V.I.P. Bonus #3

For V.I.P. Clients Only!

Give the gift that fits all...

20% Off Gift Certificates

Buy as many as you want, in any denomination you want!

Gift Certificates are valid on purchases made after January 2, 2004. Offer expires 12/24/03. SKU#32-685

Baltimore's World Class Men's Stores

Free Parking Next Door

Downtown Across from the 1st Mariner Arena
200 W. Baltimore Street
410-727-0763   Mon-Sat 9 to 6 & Sunday 11 to 4

Owings Mills in Valley Centre
9616 Reisterstown Road
410-581-5351 Mon-Sat 10 to 9 & Sunday 12 to 5

Gage   MasterCard   VISA   MOST
Verified Checks and Bank Debit Cards

www.gagemenswear.com

Join our Repeat Rewards program and save every time you shop!

Gage Menswear's offer printed inside the HOLIDAY MAILING postcard.
You can see this in full color when you claim your FREE CD
of all of the exhibits in this book by using the form on page 312.

And the payoff is that those three reasons are coupons!

> *Coupon #1* is to save on merchandise, and it even offers three different options to save depending on how much is purchased. Again, I stress that customers love options.
>
> *Coupon #2* is for a free designer pair of socks WITH ANY PURCHASE!!!
>
> *Coupon #3* is for a discount off of gift certificates. This coupon is, if the new customer likes you, the gift that keeps on giving ... to you in terms of long-term sales.

Look again at the offer and you can see that it is compelling because there is so much to it. You may not even know my store and you may have never been in Baltimore, but because of how I present this, I bet you wish you could have profited from this offer!

And as the retailer, I certainly profited from this offer. In fact, once I learned about the "power of the premium," I used them as many times as I could.

Premiums to Increase Referrals

Premiums can be used in more than just direct mail. They can and should be used in every media.

For example, several years ago I consulted with a client who was a dentist. He asked me for some advice in order to stimulate more referrals to his office.

After a bit of thought, I realized that perhaps the best time to stimulate referrals from his existing patients was when they were in the midst of having a dental procedure.

Think about it. When you're sitting in a dental chair and your dentist or his hygienist has his or her hands in your mouth, you can't move.

So in each operatory, I strategically placed a large sign on the wall where patients would have to stare at it the entire time they're in the chair. The sign would encourage them to refer their friends and family members to the dentist's office.

Dr. Ed Shaivitz's REFERRAL SIGN in his operatories. You can see this in full color when you claim your FREE CD of all of the exhibits in this book by using the form on page 312.

Beneath the sign, I had a shelf installed with three gifts displayed on it. Patients could choose from:

1. a vibrating toothbrush ($97 value);

2. an exam, x-rays, and cleaning ($150 value);

3.   a $50 gift certificate to a local Italian restaurant.

You shouldn't be surprised to hear that more people requested the certificate to the Italian restaurant than the other two premiums combined even though each of the other gifts had a much higher value.

You also shouldn't be surprised to hear that these signs tripled the referrals that patients sent to his office (and continue to do so today).

Sizzling Outrageous Summation

1)   Premiums increase response by as much as 30 percent.

2)   Perceived value of premiums is important, so make sure you tell prospects the value and show a photo with a description.

3)   Giving people a choice of premiums typically will increase response.

4)   Connecting premiums to your campaign strengthens your message.

5)   Use premiums in your OUTRAGEOUS advertising every chance you get.

9) Reminding Sequentially Until They Buy

Remembering to shop at your business might not be on the top of all your customers' to-do lists.

In fact, chances are, you've lost some customers. People simply disappear for many reasons.

These customers have purchased from you before, but for one reason or another, they haven't been back. Why not? Where did they go?

Here are the main reasons that people don't continue to do business with you (in NO particular order):

- They moved away, and it's no longer convenient to do business with you.
- They had a bad experience.
- They're "price shoppers" and found someone who provides a lower price for the same product or service.
- They no longer need your product or service.

But the number-one reason that people stop doing business with you is … THEY FORGET.

It's funny, but it's not. In fact, it's downright sad. Most businesses forget that it is not the job of the customer to remember that their business exists. And so the customers disappear because they forget that the business is still around.

These are people whom I call "lost customers"—previous customers who have not returned to your business within the period of time that you think they should.

For example, in my menswear stores, we identified lost customers as people who did not return within six months. Restaurants might identify lost customers as those who don't return within three months. An optometrist might identify a lost patient as someone who doesn't return every year.

OUTRAGEOUS exercise

Identify when someone becomes a lost customer of your specific business category.

Yet the truth is that a lost customer is just someone who hasn't been reminded enough times. That's right. Lost customers need to be reminded, and not just with a campaign that says, "Remember us?"

I am suggesting a step-by-step campaign to get to these specific customers until, finally, you have broken down as many barriers as you can.

Usually, it takes three or four steps … but it's worth it!

learn to think differently

Part of the secret to successful OUTRAGEOUS advertising is simply to learn to think differently. This happened to me, as I wrote in the preface, when I attended a marketing seminar for which Dan Kennedy was one of the speakers.

One of the things that Dan talked about that day was the concept of sequencing—sending more than one advertising message to customers over a series of time. When I first heard of this concept, my jaw dropped. It made perfect logical sense.

Not everyone thought so. My father, for instance, was still involved in the family business at the time, and I came back from that seminar and told him about the idea of mailing an offer two weeks apart to the same person. The second piece of mail would go to anyone who didn't respond to the first, I told my father.

"You're crazy," said my father. "Why would you want to waste money on people who didn't respond the first time?"

Crazy?

No, more like understanding human nature. After all, everyone is a procrastinator.

increase results ... double your response!

Whatever response you get in one mailing (or ad of any kind), you will double in three mailings. And usually, you do better than that.

It's actually simple. A lot of people will put you in the "maybe later" pile as discussed in chapter 2. And even though you've made it into that pile, you will often disappear along with everything else in that "maybe later" pile because people are busy. Remember, it's not their job to remember your business.

But by reminding them, you become more than a blip on their radar screen. You recapture their interest.

Of course, doubling your response is only really helpful if your initial response to the first advertisement was significant. After all, zero times two equals zero. Or as Dan Kennedy says: "YOU CAN'T MULTIPLY ZEROS."

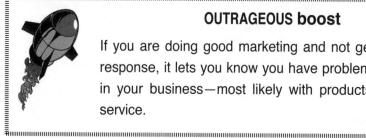

OUTRAGEOUS boost

If you are doing good marketing and not getting a good response, it lets you know you have problems elsewhere in your business—most likely with products, pricing, or service.

There are things to weigh before moving forward. Typically, a sequential campaign is worth it, but you do have to do the math. It depends on the transaction size you are getting versus the cost of continuing a campaign, plus the size of the initial response.

The mechanics of proceeding forward basically begin with a test. Trying a campaign on a core group of 500 customers will usually tell you if the OUTRAGEOUS idea you are implementing is working. From there you can expand to the entirety of your mailing list.

OUTRAGEOUS boost

Clean and update your customer list often. About 18 percent of the American population moves every year. Your customer list needs to be current in order to accurately judge results.

Once you have determined that an initial mailing is effective, you can implement the sequential portion of the campaign. This means that about ten days to two weeks later, the customers who didn't respond to the first mailing get another reminder.

dean killingbeck's cold birthday mailing

Dean Killingbeck is a former sales representative to the home and garden store industry. He is a Glazer-Kennedy member, one of our independent business advisors in Michigan, and a master marketer in his own right.

And Dean was once consulting for a restaurant when he came up with an idea of buying a list of birthdays for all women from the ages of thirty-five to sixty-five in a certain geographic area around the restaurant.

Dean merged a lot of things together in this campaign, giving it a definite theme and look—starting right off with the stamp on the first envelope.

Dean Killingbeck's birthday envelope. You can see this in full color when you claim your FREE CD of all of the exhibits in this book by using the form on page 312.

And then inside the envelope is a letter wishing a happy birthday and offering a free birthday meal. The letter uses all the essential elements and throws in extras like testimonials, personalization, and double readership.

Happy Birthday
Amanda Adcock!!
Get a FREE Birthday Dinner with
Absolutely No Strings Attached!

Happy Birthday Amanda,

A special friend of ours told us it's your birthday this month and to help you celebrate, we are buying you dinner! Just bring in the enclosed **FREE** entrée gift certificate valued to **$6.95** on or before December 31st and use it any way you want! It's your birthday and you deserve to be a VIP on your special day so come and celebrate with us at **The Brunchery Restaurant and Catering.**

What's the Catch and Why Are We Doing This?
There isn't any catch! Use your FREE $6.95 entrée gift certificate any time before December 31st with absolutely no strings attached. We are doing this because we love people to come in and celebrate their birthdays. It's a very happy and festive time and boy do we like happy people!!

What Makes Us So Special?
The Brunchery Restaurant and Catering has been serving the Tampa Bay area since 1985. We have received numerous awards and accolades, including "Best for Breakfast" by the Tampa Tribune, "Best Brunch" by South Tampa News, and "Best of South Tampa" by Reader's Choice Poll. However, when we were asked by the White House to cater when President Bush came to the Tampa Bay area, that was our biggest compliment. One of our specialties is our Signature French Toast, which is so decadent, we bet you've never tasted anything like this before! Thick Texas toast with our special cream cheese sauce, fresh strawberries, bananas, slivered almonds all topped with powdered sugar. Also, our Crab & Cream Cheese Crepes are a featured delicacy at food shows, catering events and a favorite of tourists and locals alike. Not in the mood for breakfast? We also offer salads, soups, sandwiches and burgers.

Here's What Some Of Our Guests Had To Say:
"Excellent food. Friendly helpful service. easily doable during lunch hour." Connie Davis
"Great food and service. Definitely a favorite place for dining." Juan Ricardes

Claiming your FREE Birthday Dinner is Easy.
Simply bring in your gift certificate and choose one of our many popular dishes on our menu. Whatever your craving, we are sure to satisfy your appetite here at The Brunchery Restaurant and Catering. So come on in, celebrate your birthday with us, and expect to be impressed!

Looking forward to celebrating with you!

Gregory Elliot

Gregory Elliot, Owner

P.S. Bring in your enclosed FREE Entrée Gift Certificate, valued to $6.95, anytime on or before December 31, 2006. No cost, no obligation to buy anything else. Just enjoy yourself.

15706 Dale Mabry Hwy N   Tampa, FL 33618-1608   **The Brunchery**
Phone (813) 964-8143   www.brunchery.com   Restaurant & Catering

Dean Killingbeck's birthday letter. You can see this in full color when you claim your FREE CD of all of the exhibits in this book by using the form on page 312.

184

But then, if the person still doesn't come in for the free meal, a second attempt is made with a funny postcard featuring a baby with cake all over its face. On the back of the card is a gift certificate—a reminder again that this offer is one he or she should try to remember!

Alan... We Missed You On Your Birthday!!

This is your Last Chance to get a *FREE* Birthday Dinner worth $14.00! Hurry, this offer expires 10/31/06!!

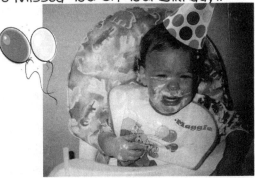

We're really upset you didn't celebrate your birthday with us!

Dean Killingbeck's birthday postcard. You can see this in full color when you claim your FREE CD of all of the exhibits in this book by using the form on page 312.

OUTRAGEOUS resource

Dean Killingbeck's company, New Customers Now, can manage the entire campaign for you to acquire new customers by buying birthday lists of your ideal prospects and mailing them out a sequence to attract them to your business using "Bill Glazer style" OUTRAGEOUS advertising. You can contact his company at www.Bill.NewCustomersNowMarketing.com.

connecting the dots

When you run a sequential campaign, you as the OUTRAGEOUS advertiser need to connect the dots. One thing needs to refer back to another, reminding the customer that "We've mailed you this offer once before."

Tying this together is an essential element for a sequential campaign to work. There are a number of creative ways to do this, as I will illustrate in the upcoming examples. But the overall point is that each step of the sequence must be tied together.

OUTRAGEOUS boost

The time between steps of a sequential campaign can vary significantly within this limit: <u>typically never more than fourteen days apart</u>. From fourteen days apart to a day apart can work in certain steps of any campaign.

In a sequential campaign, you are reaching out to customers who have already seen step one. So it is important to tie step two to step one and, while referring back to step one, give a REASON WHY you are sending this again. Customers are smart and perceptive, and yet suggestible.

farmers & merchants bank campaign

How's this for OUTRAGEOUS—a bank sending you a bank deposit bag in the mail as I showed you in chapter 8 when I used it to illustrate premiums.

The bag itself, besides being an OUTRAGEOUS way to get a sales letter into the hands of the customer, is the very beginning of getting this message of who exactly sent this to the customer.

And so with that, step one of the sequential campaign was complete, and quite successful. But the bank was not finished yet.

A second mailing was then sent out connecting the dots to the first mailing of the bank bag. This mailing was a clear plastic bag full of shredded money, and another detailed sales letter.

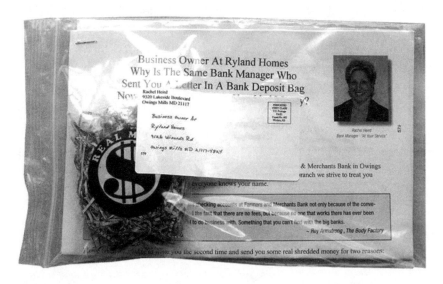

Farmers & Merchants Bank Shredded Money Mailing. You can see this in full color when you claim your FREE CD of all of the exhibits in this book by using the form on page 312.

The letter was of the same design as the letter in the bank deposit bag, with an updated headline connecting the dots of the campaign and again asking and then answering the obvious question:

"Why Is The Same Bank Manager Who You A Letter In A Bank Deposit Bag Now Sending You A Bag Of Shredded Money?"

Immediately "reason why" copy is hinted at; the dots are connected; and the campaign reminds the customers that they've seen something like this before. This is important because it triggers that "maybe later" memory that you are trying to access and turn into "I want this."

Finally, the third mailing was a pop-up envelope that again connected the dots and was OUTRAGEOUS in its own way.

Farmers & Merchants Bank Pop-Up Envelope. You can see this in full color when you claim your FREE CD of all of the exhibits in this book by using the form on page 312.

This had a coupon for one of the six premiums actually attached to the inside flap of the envelope. This made it so that as soon as you opened it, without even reaching inside, you had access to the coupon.

As you can see, the bank followed up three times to create a very successful campaign in order to attract new customers. And I can tell you that if they just sent out one mailing, the results they achieved wouldn't have been nearly as good.

how many in the sequence?

The idea of doubling your response in three mailings is obviously intriguing.

But why stop there?

Why indeed! In fact, I have used up to fourteen steps in my sequential marketing to promote my Platinum Business Building Marketing System (bgsmarketing.com) through the years—although I did scale that campaign back to a mere nine steps. In other words, keep going until it doesn't work anymore. Some people just need to be reminded a lot or until they are finally ready to buy.

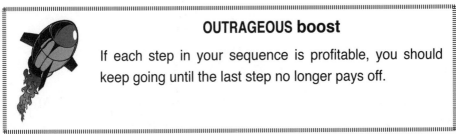

OUTRAGEOUS boost

If each step in your sequence is profitable, you should keep going until the last step no longer pays off.

diversity leads to stability

There are lots of ways to put together a sequence. And there is different media—various ways to time and sequence things together.

If you remember, Yanik Silver's "Save Yanik's Marriage" campaign started with an e-mail, and it directed you to a Web page.

So for instance, you can start with a piece of mail and then follow it with a phone message and an e-mail. Each is a different media. The reason to do this is that every one of your customers has different media habits, but if you reach into enough different media formats, you are going to find them.

And then, by using sequential reminders to refer back to previous media messages, the dots will be connected to the point where the customer finally gives in and says, "I really have to go do business with these people."

thanksgiving sequence

Have you ever received a holiday card in December from a business? Of course, you have received a bunch of these through the years—competing with personal holiday greeting cards from friends and family.

Are holiday cards in December easy to ignore?

YES!

Does sending a holiday card in December resemble something OUTRAGEOUS?

NO!!!

But ...

What if you sent a greeting card at another time of year, when no one else is sending them?

Well, I have a solution. I send out Thanksgiving greeting cards. After all, what better time to send out a greeting card to one of your best customers/clients/patients than Thanksgiving, the holiday when we give thanks. And besides, very few people send out Thanksgiving cards, so you won't be lost in the clutter of cards.

It takes time and effort to grow a great business relationship. I'm grateful for the part you've played in growing ours.
Happy Thanksgiving!

(Your company's personalization here. Maximum 45 letters and spaces per line.)

Front And Inside Message Of Thanksgiving Greeting Card.
You can see this in full color when you claim your FREE CD of all of the exhibits in this book by using the form on page 312.

Check it out: A turkey with a sign that says "Eat Ham." Now that's funny, OUTRAGEOUS, and it gets attention!

I started doing this at my menswear store, and I discovered that when you pick a different holiday to send out greeting cards, the cards you send actually get attention. And sending a Thanksgiving card gives you built-in "reason why" copy—you can thank your customers.

Plus, sending a Thanksgiving card has an extra bonus of arriving the week of the busiest shopping day of the year—the day after Thanksgiving. All those people are shopping anyway. They may as well think of your business! After all, the best time to target people is when they already are in the mood to buy.

OUTRAGEOUS resource

The Thanksgiving greeting card promotion works great for every type of business including professional practices, B2B, service businesses, retail, sales organizations, restaurants, etc., etc.

If you are interested in getting these cards to send from your own business, call BGS Marketing at 1-800-545-0414 and leave a message. A customer service representative will return your call within forty-eight hours Monday–Friday.

But a Thanksgiving card was only part of a quick multi-media campaign.

The card itself is typically sent out on a Saturday so that it arrives at the customer's house on Tuesday before Thanksgiving. Inside the card is an insert telling the reader to ...

PLEASE OPEN THIS IMMEDIATELY

(EVEN BEFORE YOU PLACE THIS THANKSGIVING CARD ON DISPLAY)

As you can imagine, the recipient is so curious with the above message that he or she opens it up immediately, and inside is a special incentive to do business with you.

But that is just step one of maximizing this Thanksgiving weekend promotion. For the first five years I used these cards, I stopped at the first step. And then one year, after hearing Reid Hoisington, a marketer to the mortgage industry, at one of Dan Kennedy's Mastermind meetings, talk about voice mail, I added a couple extra steps.

On Wednesday, before Thanksgiving, I left a voice mail on the customer's answering machine. This is the same customer who received the Thanksgiving greeting card, and now I was wishing him or her a nice holiday and reminding him or her of the offer on the insert that accompanied the card.

Thanksgiving Greeting Card Voice Broadcast Script:

Hi, this is (your name), owner of (name of your store). I hope by now you've received the Thanksgiving card we sent you. I really appreciate your business. As a way of showing our thanks, don't forget to bring in the enclosed Special Certificate for our Customer Appreciation Days this Friday, Saturday, Sunday, and Monday.

Remember, as a preferred (name of your store) client, you are eligible for up to 18 percent off your purchase, and if you bring a friend or relative, I'll give you both a full 20 percent off your purchases.

Again, Customer Appreciation Days are this Friday through Monday only. If you have any questions, please call us at (your phone number). By the way, if you lost your certificate, just mention codeword TURKEY and I'll give you another one in the store.

On behalf of the entire (name of your store) family, I hope you and yours have a safe and happy Thanksgiving!

OUTRAGEOUS resource

Below are the names of a couple companies you can contact to provide voice broadcast for your company:

- AMS at http://www.automatedmarketingsolutions. com/broadcasting
- Arch Telecom at http://archtelecom.com/products/ voice_broadcast/index.asp

When an answering machine picked up, my voice, sounding as if I called this machine myself, was on the line. And later, when I was in the store during the sale, many people actually came up to me and remarked how nice it was for me to call them and remind them of this sale.

Plus—the best part—adding step two in a different media to the sequence increased response to 92 percent!

what i did in 2000; taking advantage of a news event

Thanksgiving in the year 2000 was an interesting time in the USA. If anyone remembers, there was a very tight presidential election that year, and by Thanksgiving, the race between George W. Bush and Al Gore had still not been decided because they were recounting the votes in Florida.

So that year I added a twist to the voice broadcast as part of the sequential campaign featuring a celebrity impersonator voice delivering a message from President Bill Clinton.

Bill Clinton impersonator voice broadcast script. You can hear this and other r ecordings mentioned in this book when you request the free OUTRAGEOUS CD-ROM.

Bill Clinton Impersonator

Hi there. This is NOT your president. But the president of Gage Menswear, Bill Glazer, asked me to give you a call to tell one important thing: Happy

Thanksgiving to you and your family and friends. I'm sure by now that you've received the holiday card Gage Menswear sent you. You know, they feel your pain when it comes to paying way too much for great men's clothing. So this Friday, they're kicking off their customer appreciation event, and with the coupon Bill sent you inside your card, you can save up to 20 percent off your entire purchase. And, get a free large display calculator, valued at $20. Wish I had one of those for the Oval Office. If you can't find your coupon, don't worry; just come into either store and say the code word "Bubba" and they'll give you one free. On behalf of everyone at Gage, have a wonderful holiday tomorrow, and they'll see you Friday through Monday at Gage Menswear.

WOW! This twist increased response another 21 percent over the previous year!

Since this was so much fun, the next year I delivered a message from an Arnold Schwarzenegger impersonator as Governor Terminator.

Arnold Schwarzenegger impersonator voice broadcast script. *You can hear this and other recordings mentioned in this book when you request the free OUTRAGEOUS CD-ROM.*

Arnold Impersonator

Hello, this is Arnold from California. You know, Governor Terminator? I'm checking in again to make sure you had a wonderful Thanksgiving and to remind you that it's imperative that your plans for this weekend include getting over to Gage Menswear. Bill Glazer is making a Herculean effort to stimulate the economy by lowering all his prices. In addition, he is giving nineteen dollars and forty-six cents toward any purchase, free, no strings attached from now until Monday. This will terminate shopping debt. Don't forget a terrific holiday gift suggestion from my lovely wife, Maria—Gage gift certificates. Stop into Gage and bring the money-saving certificate. You might even see me. They have my size and yours too. Don't forget to pick up your two free gifts. Just use the code word "Terminator." The locations are excellent—downtown and Owings Mills. I'll be back, at Gage Menswear. They are open all weekend.

OUTRAGEOUS resource

Contact Mike DeJesus for hundreds of famous voice impersonations at mhaze993@aol.com or (413)297-3676 or (413)562-1566.

In later years I also added e-mail marketing as a step in the Thanksgiving greeting card promotion, which not only added another media (diversity leads to stability) but also increased overall response.

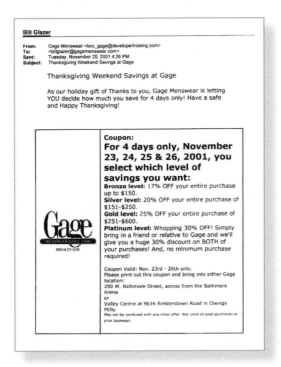

Gage Menswear's Thanksgiving greeting cards e-mail reminder.

specifically targeting lost customers

Every business has lost customers, and you should NOT ignore them. The fact is they are the third easiest customers to sell—only third to

1) active customers;

2) referrals.

Once again, lost customers are customers who have bought from you in the past but have NOT come back in the amount of time that you would have expected.

So what do you do?

Well, the first thing you want to do is make sure your customer list is clean and up to date. Then you want to let them know they are lost and you miss seeing them. Remember it's not the job of the customer to remember you. It's your job to remind them of the products and services you provide.

The second step is to place these customers into a sequential campaign because lost customers typically take a little more work in order to get them to return.

OUTRAGEOUS **boost**

The first step in pursuing lost customers is to be sure your customer list is clean and up to date.

For example, let me show you the four-step sequence that I used in my menswear stores in order to attract back lost customers. In fact, this campaign never delivered less than 13 percent of these customers back to my store.

I'm not sure if you're impressed with this 13 percent statistic, but you should be. The 13 percent represented hundreds of thousands of dollars in "lost" revenue each year, and it also represented a return of hundreds of customers that we would have otherwise lost for good.

the gage lost customer campaign

At my menswear store, we tested several lost customer campaigns throughout the years and found that a four-step campaign, which included three oversized postcards and a voice broadcast, was the winner.

The first oversized postcard had a picture of a dangling carrot on it.

Gage Menswear's step #1, front and back of the lost customer "dangling carrot" postcard. You can see this in full color when you claim your FREE CD of all of the exhibits in this book by using the form on page 312.

And the message is clearly, with a handwritten headline, that **We Miss You.**

The carrot is there as a visual way of telling them something is there for them. And immediately, there is "reason why" copy: "Our records indicate it's been too long since you've visited Gage Menswear."

From there, you see an offer, a deadline, and—referring to that big carrot—an offer of a gift certificate that becomes a bigger discount when a purchase is made.

And on the back of the postcard is the actual coupon. Plus there is handwritten personalization and the addresses of the stores and other pertinent information.

And that was the first mail in the campaign.

But I learned that although response was pretty good on step one (about 4 percent) there were a lot more people to bring back if I continued. So I sent postcard number two, featuring a compass and a headline wondering if we should send out a search party ...

Immediately, the dots are connected with the first sentence that begins, "A few weeks ago, we mailed you ..."

And the second sentence—giving a reason why—begins, "Well in case you misplaced it, here's another one ..."

And the compass replaces the carrot, but the offer remains the same, and the deadline is moved, and you are urged to flip the card over.

This time, the back also has personalization—but with typewritten easiest-to-read font and a big coupon. The layout should look familiar— again connecting the dots.

Gage Menswear's step #2, front and back of the lost customer "compass" postcard.
You can see this in full color when you claim your FREE CD
of all of the exhibits in this book by using the form on page 312.

Of course, by this point, it would be easy for most companies to just quit and give up the customer to the ether of lost commerce. But not all companies—and not my company!

You see, I knew better. So before I quit, I told the customers I was going to quit. I sent them a "last chance" postcard that used "Last Chance" as a headline and then pictured a legal pad with the words "WE QUIT!" written on it.

***Gage Menswear's step #3**, front and back of the lost customer "We Quit" postcard. You can see this in full color when you claim your FREE CD of all of the exhibits in this book by using the form on page 312.*

Right under the "WE QUIT!" headline is "reason why" copy, starting with, "Twice before we mailed you ..."

And then, the offer again looks similar to the previous two postcards. And on the back is more personalization and "last chance" messaging, and then there is the same coupon as the previous two postcards.

By then, for sure, others would have given up. Not me. Not this campaign!

The fourth and final step was a voice mail from me, the owner. People like to hear from the owner, and, as the owner of Gage Menswear, I was always happy to send a voice mail. Especially because I knew even a final effort, using a different media, would still bring some response.

Gage Menswear's step #4, lost customer campaign voice broadcast script.
You can hear this and other recordings mentioned in this book when you request the free OUTRAGEOUS CD-ROM.

Hi, this is (owner/manager/key employee name) from (name of your store). We recently sent you three postcards with (your offer). We really do want you back as a customer. Please bring in your (offer) before (expiration date). If you can't find your postcards, that's okay. Simply come into the store and say codeword (codeword) and we'll still give you (the offer).

Looking forward to seeing you in (name of your store) before (expiration date)!

As you can clearly see, this is a very smart strategy for any business, and you should put some thought into how you will structure your own lost customer campaign ... but I URGE you to put one in place.

Remember, these are the third easiest customers/clients/patients to sell, and the number-one reason why they probably haven't continued to do business with you is they have simply forgotten to do so.

OUTRAGEOUS boost

If customers do not respond to a lost customer campaign, you should not forget about them. I'd suggest you put them through "at least" one more campaign in six months before you decide on finally removing them from your database.

S.O.S.

Sizzling Outrageous Summation

1) Every business has lost customers.

2) It is not your customers' job to remember your business. It is your job to remind them about your products and services.

3) If you run a sequential campaign to lost customers, you can double your response.

4) Keep your customer list clean to best gauge results.

5) A sequential campaign must connect the marketing; each step should refer to the previous ones.

6) Run a sequence until it doesn't work anymore.

7) Diversity leads to stability: a sequence in more than one media is most effective.

10) Swiping Ideas And Deploying Them Into Your Business

One year, a friend of mine sent me a box of Omaha Steaks as a gift. They were great steaks, and every year since then, I have been on their mailing list.

At the time of this particular story, I was operating my menswear stores. Omaha Steaks were selling steaks. What could I possibly learn from them?

How about a great idea? See, shortly after I received the box of steaks as a gift, I got on Omaha Steaks' mailing list and an envelope arrived from them in my pile of mail.

Instead of just being an envelope, it was what I call a pop-up envelope, where there's an actual coupon attached to the back of the flap in the inside.

So, as soon as I opened up the envelope, the coupon popped up for savings on an order for more steaks. As soon as I saw this, I said to myself, "This is great. I don't even have to hunt for an offer."

Then I immediately did something else. I called my printer and asked if there was any way that I could do this. Not for steaks, mind you. I was still selling menswear. I just wanted to copy the concept of a pop-up envelope.

That's right, my best ideas aren't mine. They are borrowed.

The phrase I use is "S&D" (swipe and deploy). The idea of S&D marketing is that every idea out there is fair game for me to take and adjust to use to my advantage. In fact, I encourage you to do that with everything in this book.

Front

Back

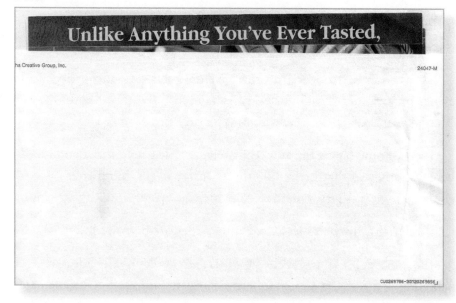

Front and back of Omaha Steaks' pop-up envelope. You can see this in full color when
you claim your FREE CD of many of the exhibits in this book by using the form on page 312.

But here's the right and ethical way to do this. Look outside your industry. The best ideas to S&D aren't going to come from copying what your competitors are doing. And, in fact, doing so is actually unethical. Instead, find someone doing something else in another industry and see if you can make his or her ideas work for you.

first, avoid unethical s&d

Borrow, but don't borrow exactly word for word. Remember the "deploy" part of S&D.

In other words, if you are in the same business as I am and in the same market, do more than take my logo off of my advertisements and slap yours on. Copying in such a blatant fashion is unethical—and it will probably backfire, as customers in the same market could recognize the campaign from another business and punish you for it.

Stealing the ideas of your direct competition is unethical even if the customers don't call you on it. It's just wrong. But even more, it's not nearly as effective as importing and tweaking an idea from another industry.

When you take an idea from anywhere, tweak the words a little—as you will be forced to do to ethically S&D in order to make it suit your business.

the many sources of ethical s&d

Look, S&D is ethical. I just had to warn you in that previous section not to steal directly from your direct competition.

On the other hand, if an idea has worked somewhere else, it will probably work for you. Good ideas translate easily into a second use across industries, and once you learn this simple concept, you will realize that S&D is easy, ethical, and it works.

So if you are going to swipe and deploy for your own business, where do you look to swipe? Well … everywhere!

Your eyes should be open to everything and anything, and at least one compartment of your mind needs to be in a constant state of marketing. Stay interested, stay curious. Look at everything!

the top three sources to s&d

You can find ideas anywhere, but some places are naturally more fertile than others. And it doesn't matter who you are or what business you are in, once you start looking in these three areas, you will find a wealth of ideas.

#1 - Your Own Mailbox

You are not the only business in the world that is trying to sell something. If you look around the world, you will see that you are inundated with sales messages. But you don't even have to venture into the world to find what I think is the best source of great ideas: YOUR OWN MAILBOX.

Of course, in order to find things in your own mailbox, you have to be sure to get to the mail before it is sorted and thrown out. You, like me, may not live alone. I am married, and my wife usually gets to the mail before me.

And I believe that I am like most every other husband in America in that by the time I get to the mail, my wife has already been through it and sorted it. She has her own interpretation of A pile, B pile, and C pile. Some of it is important. Some of it we have no use for. And some is to be looked at later.

Except ...

I have a use for ALL of it.

You see, even if you have no interest in responding at all to an offer, it's still worth carefully studying. It's like having a mini-marketing lesson every day for FREE!

You want to study:

- What others are doing
- How they are doing it
- How they're trying to grab your attention

When something comes into your mailbox, even if it is a bad campaign, you can use it as an opportunity to observe and even learn.

And sometimes, you just might see something that is great and be able to swipe and then deploy.

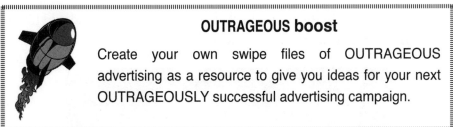

OUTRAGEOUS boost

Create your own swipe files of OUTRAGEOUS advertising as a resource to give you ideas for your next OUTRAGEOUSLY successful advertising campaign.

#2 Referrals

I'll guarantee this will happen to you. Once you start using more and more OUTRAGEOUS advertising, people will remember you as the person who does OUTRAGEOUS advertising.

Since people love this stuff, you will inevitably have something like fans—people who are on your side and love your advertising so much that they are actually on the lookout for similar, or at least interesting, advertising to show you.

"Hey, you've got to see this," they'll say.

The true magic of this type of advertising is that it is actually memorable and interesting and therefore noticeable, and since it is all of those things, you end up developing a sort of silent army of admirers who will speak up from time to time when they see something that they think may interest you. These people are a tremendous resource.

It happens to me all the time. For instance, I have a friend who owns a local Ford dealership, and he recently sent me a terrific example of OUTRAGEOUS advertising that he received in the mail because he knew I would enjoy seeing it and perhaps want to S&D it.

It was a tin box with a window in it that contained a pair of special glasses and a sheet of paper containing his own personal URL (with his name written in it) for him to type into the browser of his computer and look at while wearing the special glasses.

When he typed in the URL, the Web site welcomed him and told him to put on the glasses to see the rest of the message. How cool is that?!?!?!

3-D sunglasses mailing. You can see this in full color when you claim your FREE CD of many of the exhibits in this book by using the form on page 312.

Now I haven't figured out yet how I will S&D this, but it immediately went into my special box where I keep all this stuff for future reference. You can bet that I'll figure out a great use for this.

OUTRAGEOUS boost

Notify your friends that you are always on the lookout for OUTRAGEOUS advertising that grabs their attention and ask them to save it for you whenever they come across something.

#3 – All Media

Everything is fair game.

Whenever you are exposed to any category of media, always pay attention. Don't make the mistake of thinking that you can only S&D a direct mail idea for direct mail.

Anything is fair game. You might see something while watching TV and say, "This is great; I've got to S&D this and figure out how to use it for an OUTRAGEOUS billboard."

So, if it's a radio ad, don't change the station. Same with a fax you receive in your office, or an Internet site. Even if you are not interested in what they are selling, pay attention to how they are selling it … especially if they've grabbed your attention by doing something OUTRAGEOUS. There's a good chance that there's something in this idea that you can use.

There are amazing ideas out there just waiting for your S&D tweaks, and they are all over every imaginable media. All that you have to do is pay attention and you'll see how fun and easy this is to do.

example #1 - the crayon letter

Sometimes you see an idea and you automatically know it's great. This happened to me in December 2003 when I received Dan Kennedy's No-BS Marketing letter highlighting a campaign sent out by one of his subscribers, Buffy Dupont, who worked with her husband at his auto repair shop.

OUTRAGEOUS resource

You can subscribe to a free two-month trial of Dan Kennedy's No BS Marketing Letter and test-drive over $600 of marketing and money-making information at www. dankennedy.com.

The campaign Buffy Dupont used with great success was a letter to customers from her seven-year-old daughter.

It wasn't just any letter. It was written in crayon.

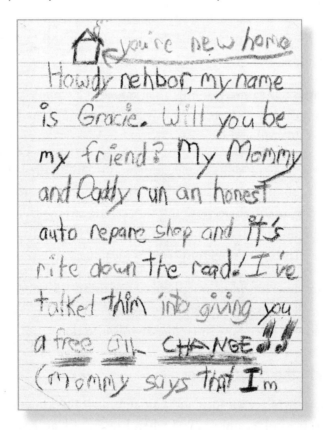

Buffy Dupont's Crayon Letter. You can see this in full color when you claim your FREE CD of many of the exhibits in this book by using the form on page 312.

A letter written in different color crayons with words misspelled the way a seven-year-old child would write it, asking, "Would you like to come into my Daddy's shop to get a free oil change?" was something that I noticed immediately. I knew it was a great idea, and I had to figure out a way to S&D it.

But I also knew that, as executed, it was a great idea for Buffy Dupont. You see, she had a real seven-year-old daughter. This made it a believable letter. It had "reason why" copy—and an actual story of a real child behind it.

At the time, I had an eighteen-year-old daughter and a twenty-one-year-old son. Obviously, their crayon days were long behind them. And they weren't getting younger.

But I knew there had to be a way to make it work, and then, when I realized how a simple twist could make it work, I was ready to spring into action. I knew better than to immediately disqualify such a good idea. There had to be a way.

Sure, my son, Josh, was twenty-one. But … he wasn't always twenty-one.

And that was it. There it was—an idea was born, and Josh suddenly had written a crayon letter when he was six and he made me promise that when he graduated from college … well, check it out.

Outside Of Josh Glazer's Crayon Letter. You can see this in full color when you claim your FREE CD of many of the exhibits in this book by using the form on page 312.

Tweaking this idea to make a crayon letter work for my twenty-one-year-old son was all it took to swipe this idea and deploy it into my own business. I actually did a lot more tweaking, but this tweak on the sales idea itself turned it into an original-enough piece to make it work for me.

And on the inside is an actual photo of my twenty-one-year-old son and me standing together on his graduation day. And the letter itself is from "Josh Glazer's proud Dad."

And you see immediately my "reason why" copy of "Making Good On The Promise I Made To My Son Over Fifteen Years Ago!"

In the letter, I tell the story of the promise that I made to my son fifteen years earlier, which was the reason for the offer, and of course there was a deadline.

Then continuing with the theme of the campaign, I include a coupon for a premium of a free umbrella, and I call this "Josh's Gift To You."

Inside Of Josh Glazer's Crayon Letter. You can see this in full color when you claim your FREE CD of many of the exhibits in this book by using the form on page 312.

This campaign, which was a pure S&D endeavor inspired by Buffy Dupont's letter, generated $23 in sales for every dollar we spent. Yes, crayons work wonders.

example # 2 – omaha steaks

At the beginning of this chapter I began to tell the story of the pop-up envelope with a coupon on the back that I received from Omaha Steaks and how I had to call my printer to see if I could duplicate the idea.

The truth is that I couldn't duplicate the idea. Omaha Steaks is a huge company that sent out thousands of mailings, and their huge volume was the only way they could afford such an intricate mailing. How did I know? I called the printer that printed up the mailing for Omaha Steaks and asked them what they charged.

OUTRAGEOUS resource

You can get pop-up mailings done by City Print USA:
Contact Steve Harshbarger
Phone: 1-866-907-1222
E-mail: sales@cityprintusa.com

But I didn't let this bit of news discourage me. Instead, I called the printer I typically used and he came up with a similar idea with a lot less complicated execution and at one-quarter the cost.

At the time, I was looking for a New Year's Day promotion for my menswear retail stores, and since it was for the year 2001, I came up with a "no-strings-attached" gift certificate for $20.04.

OUTRAGEOUS boost

When you make a no-strings-attached offer, very few will take advantage of you. In fact, most people spend a multiple of what you are giving away for free. This is called the law of reciprocity, and it is very real.

This was a New Year's Day special, and we were swamped with people. In fact, this was the second most effective campaign (next to the five-page sales letter, see chapter 1) that I ever ran.

Gage Menswear's 2001 New Year's Day pop-up envelope. *You can see this in full color when you claim your FREE CD of many of the exhibits in this book by using the form on page 312.*

And then, to show the power of S&D, a company that prepares tax returns, headquartered in Virginia, took the same pop-up envelope idea and tweaked it again and made it work for that business.

This is a great example of the power of what I call S&D marketing. You've just seen how an OUTRAGEOUS idea can be used for three different companies that on the surface have nothing in common—from selling steaks to selling menswear to selling tax returns.

Pro-Tax pop-up envelope. *You can see this in full color when you claim your FREE CD of many of the exhibits in this book by using the form on page 312.*

OUTRAGEOUS exercise

Since the pop-up envelope places its offer right in front of a customer or prospect as soon as he or she lifts the flap, this is a great promotion to use when you have a truly great offer. Develop the most generous (and OUTRAGEOUS) offer you can think of for your products or services.

example #3 – x-ray mailing

In the spectrum of A pile, B pile, and C pile, medical results including x-rays and the like would certainly end up in the A pile. After all, I think you'll agree that medical results need to be opened now.

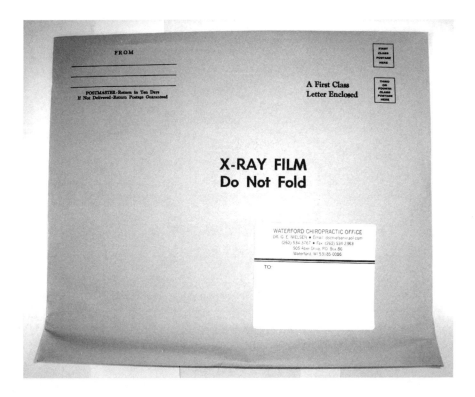

FROM

POSTMASTER-Return in Ten Days
If Not Delivered-Return Postage Guaranteed

FIRST
CLASS
POSTAGE
HERE

**A First Class
Letter Enclosed**

THIRD
OR
FOURTH
CLASS
POSTAGE
HERE

**X-RAY FILM
Do Not Fold**

WATERFORD CHIROPRACTIC OFFICE
DR. G. E. NIELSEN • Email dochnielsen@aol.com
(262) 534-3767 • Fax (262) 534-2363
505 Aber Drive, PO Box 86
Waterford, WI 53185-0086

TO:

Front Of Dr. Greg Nielsen's X-Ray Mailing Envelope. You can see this in full color when you claim your FREE CD of many of the exhibits in this book by using the form on page 312.

Well, Dr. Greg Nielsen, a chiropractor, knows this, and he came up with a brilliant marketing technique built on this concept. For a campaign, he had his staff send out x-rays of his own yellow pages ad and a letter inside from the staff.

The letter included "reason why" copy—that they mistakenly x-rayed their yellow pages ad and now didn't know what to do with them.

So, they decided to mail the 100 copies of the mistaken x-rays that they created along with a prescription for a free office visit to 100 of their past patients.

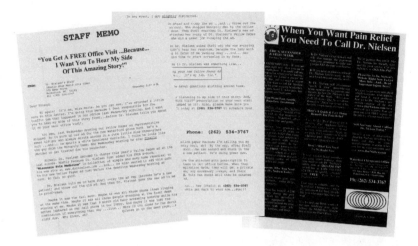

Staff memo and x-ray from Dr. Greg Nielsen's x-ray mailing.
You can see this in full color when you claim your FREE CD
of many of the exhibits in this book by using the form on page 312.

I thought this was a brilliant campaign. In fact, I liked it so much ... you guessed it, I just had to S&D it.

WATERFORD CHIROPRACTIC OFFICE
DR. G.E. NIELSEN • DOCNIELSEN@AOL.COM
505 ABER DRIVE, P.O. BOX 86
WATERFORD, WI 53185-0086

PHONE: (262) 534-3767   FAX: (262) 534-2363

_____   _____
(PATIENT'S NAME)   (DATE)

Rx: *One Free Office Visit*

_____   EXPIRES: _____
(DOCTOR'S SIGNATURE)

Prescription coupon inserted inside Dr. Nielsen's x-ray mailing.
You can see this in full color when you claim your FREE CD
of many of the exhibits in this book by using the form on page 312.

I only had a slight problem. Hopefully you figured it out by now. I am NOT a doctor.

So I had to come up with a way to S&D Dr. Nielsen's brilliantly done x-ray mailing from a menswear store owner.

After giving it about thirty-three seconds of thought, for the purpose of my x-ray mailing I became Dr. Bill Glazer, DDS. Of course, when you see DDS after a person's name, you automatically assume it is Doctor of Dental Surgery. But not me. I was Dr. Bill Glazer, DDS ... aka Doctor of **D**iscount **D**esigner **S**uits.

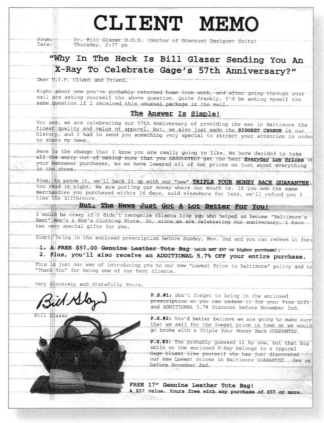

Gage Menswear Client Memo Inside The X-Ray Mailing.
You can see this in full color when you claim your FREE CD
of many of the exhibits in this book by using the form on page 312.

And the x-ray I sent out was of a big smile—the typical smile of a satisfied Gage customer.

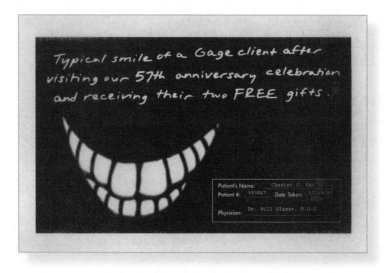

Gage Menswear x-ray inserted inside mailing. *You can see this in full color when you claim your FREE CD of many of the exhibits in this book by using the form on page 312.*

Plus I combined this with our 57th anniversary campaign—giving a 5.7 percent discount and a free tote bag, which was a $57 value.

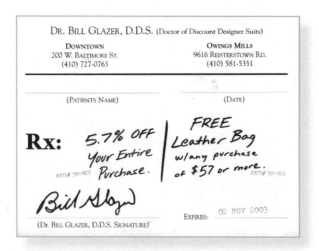

Gage Menswear prescription savings coupon. *You can see this in full color when you claim your FREE CD of many of the exhibits in this book by using the form on page 312.*

Sure, it took a bit of tweaking to make the x-ray campaign work for my menswear store. But I proved that with a bit of imagination I could transfer a great idea across industries and find success.

Of course this idea would only work for chiropractic offices or menswear stores ... right?

WRONG!

You can S&D it for just about any business if you put your mind to it.

For example, Rory Fatt, a marketing consultant to the restaurant industry, used the same idea of sending an x-ray of a smile to his customers. He cited the fact that people who attended his boot camp earned an extra $65,000 in six months, and then he asked, "Would an extra $65,000 in six months make you smile?"

Rory Fatt's S&D of the x-ray mailing that he used to sell seats to one of his seminars. You can see this in full color when you claim your FREE CD of many of the exhibits in this book by using the form on page 312.

This is yet another example of a great idea that traveled with great success across many industries.

example #4 – pill bottle mailing

Another example of a campaign that on first glance might appear to be specific to the medical industry is the pill bottle mailer.

You know, a pill bottle, just like you get prescriptions in. And again, Dr. Greg Nielsen was the first person I saw use this idea.

OUTRAGEOUS boost

When you find people who do great OUTRAGEOUS advertising, ask if they will put you on their mailing list so you can see everything new that they are doing. I've been on Dr. Nielsen's mailing list for years as he's been on mine. This is a great way to get new OUTRAGEOUS ideas.

His was a good campaign. Of course, a prescription bottle in the mail is something you have to open.

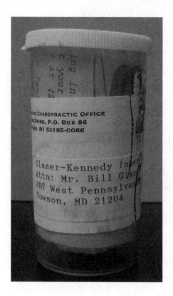

Dr. Greg Nielsen's pill bottle mailing.
You can see this in full color when you claim your FREE CD of many of the exhibits in this book by using the form on page 312.

On the inside of his prescription bottle was a tiny yo-yo with a letter from Marie in Dr. Nielsen's office asking if you wanted a prescription to stop your health problems from going up and down like a yo-yo.

This was a good campaign. The yo-yo was not perfectly connected to the pill bottle, but it was still effective, and when I saw it, I immediately liked the idea.

OUTRAGEOUS resource

Information about the pill bottle mailers is available at www.pharmacyautomationsupplies.com.

I am not the only person who liked this campaign. Nina Herschbeger, a marketing consultant, used the pill bottle mailer to send out a mini newsletter asking people to subscribe to her regular newsletter.

And then Bill Marvin, a consultant to the restaurant industry who calls himself "The Restaurant Doctor," sent out a pill bottle with a letter inside highlighted by a headline: "Where does it hurt?"

Also inside he included two aspirin, a list of possible symptoms, and then a prescription for two and a half days at his seminar.

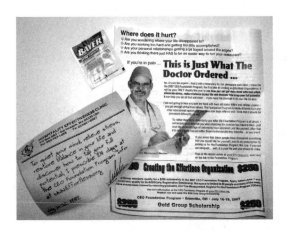

Bill Marvin's letter inside his pill bottle mailing.
You can see this in full color when you claim your FREE CD of many of the exhibits in this book by using the form on page 312.

Each generation of use of this idea created a different and almost unique version of this catchy idea. At the risk of sounding redundant, this is a great example of how you can S&D from one unrelated industry to another ... which is the BIGGEST point of this chapter.

example #5 – file folder mailing

A file folder in the mail? What's kept in a file folder? Well, important information!

So if you get a file folder in the mail, you have to see what's inside.

Examples of file folder mailings used by three people in completely unrelated industries. You can see this in full color when you claim your FREE CD of many of the exhibits in this book by using the form on page 312.

Plus, a file folder has size. It's not a typical white envelope; it's 11½ by 9½ inches. That's big. You'll notice it in your mailbox.

Nina Herschbeger, a marketing consultant, started using this idea with great success, and soon it found its way into other industries.

Dr. Greg Nielsen, a chiropractor, then used the file folder to market his practice, and then Dr. Tom Orent, a dentist who helps other dentists build their practices, used it.

Dr. Tom Orent included his photo and handwritten notes all over the inside sales letter so that it really does have the appearance of coming from a doctor.

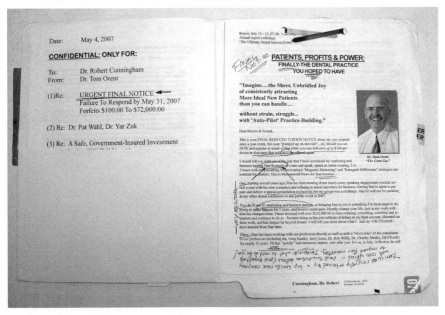

The inside of Tom Orent's file folder mailing. *You can see this in full color when you claim your FREE CD of many of the exhibits in this book by using the form on page 312.*

This execution of the idea by Dr. Orent was tremendous use of "reason why" copy by making it a confidential offer, and then all the elements of a deadline and offer are clearly visible.

Ideas, as Dr. Orent and others throughout this chapter have shown, are readily available. Just look back in previous chapters and keep reading for more.

OUTRAGEOUS exercise

Now that you've seen some terrific examples of S&D marketing and how they were transferred from one unrelated industry to another, take each of the above examples and determine how you can S&D them for your business.

1. Crayon Letter: _____

_____

_____

_____

2. Pop-Up Envelope: _____

_____

_____

_____

3. X-Ray Mailing: _____

_____

_____

_____

4. Pill Bottle Mailing: _____

_____

_____

_____

5. File Folder Mailing: _____

_____

_____

_____

Sizzling Outrageous Summation

1) Swiping and deploying great ideas is the easiest way to get ideas. If it works somewhere else, it will probably work for you.

2) Don't borrow exactly word for word from someone in your industry and market. That is unethical.

3) Ideas are everywhere.

4) The three best places to get ideas are your own mailbox, referrals, and all media.

5) Don't immediately disqualify an idea just because it seems like it doesn't fit. Chances are you can make it fit and do it brilliantly.

11) Celebrating Holidays & Special Occasions

I celebrate Leap Day.

That's right, I celebrate the extra day in February that comes around once every four years. It's an extra day! Why wouldn't you celebrate ... especially when you can use it as an excuse to make an offer to your customers?

Well, in my menswear business, I used to invite my customers to celebrate right along with me, and I found that it was a successful, fun promotion that benefited my customers as well as my store.

I sent out a postcard once every four years to tell customers I was celebrating Leap Day, and since it was an extra day, I looked upon it as a free rent day. And I wanted to share my good fortune with my customers, so I offered them 29 percent off (only on February 29th) of anything they bought on that day.

You might not have thought of Leap Day as something to celebrate. But you should now. More important, you should remember that the year is full of events to celebrate and your OUTRAGEOUS advertising should take full advantage of the special days on the calendar.

why people respond better to holidays & special occasions

People always respond to what's already on their minds.

What's on your mind? Well, what time of year is it?

You see, if it's the middle of October, you've probably at least thought of Halloween. And if it's early February, you are most likely thinking of Valentine's Day.

And that's why people respond better to special occasions. They are already thinking of them.

Robert Collier, one of the godfathers of direct-response marketing, is famous for having said, "You always want to enter the conversation already happening in someone's mind."

In other words, they're already thinking of the approaching holiday, so you may as well be part of their thinking.

Others are, in fact, enforcing this idea, so joining into that conversation every time you can is a smart decision.

the power of the anniversary promotion

The anniversary of your business is not necessarily on your customers' minds. In fact, it isn't on their minds at all because they probably don't even know when it is.

But ...

Your business's anniversary is a great reason to hold an event because it is a believable reason for you to communicate with them and to make them an offer in celebration of it.

OUTRAGEOUS boost

Even more believable than anniversaries are milestone anniversaries—5 years, 10 years, 15 years, 20, 25, 50, etc. These are special and extra believable.

Customers and prospects have been conditioned to do so. Others are already reminding people that the anniversary events are legitimate. You see them all the time. Businesses often hold anniversary events, and customers accept them as legitimate. This is your "reason why."

the top four holidays

You should celebrate every chance you can, but there are four holidays that should be at the top of your radar screen.

1) Christmas. This season seems to start as early as October, and if you have a reason at all to take advantage of it, you should remember that almost everyone gets and gives presents in December.

2) Halloween. Boo! No, it's not scary, but it offers a million opportunities to take advantage of this day of ghouls and goblins and dress-up and candy. In fact, it is the second most celebrated holiday.

3) Valentine's Day. Love is a wonderful selling point, and Valentine's Day is an actual must-buy-something holiday for anyone in a relationship or even trying to get into one. With all those lovers on the loose, you have an audience waiting to hear your message.

4) Mother's Day. Good old … "MOM." 'Nuff said. But I'll say more anyway because Mother's Day is, again, a must-buy holiday. Not all businesses can tap into this holiday, but a lot more can than think they can.

yanik silver's succinct marketing planning calendar

Yanik Silver, an online marketing expert mentioned many times in this book, has drawn up a succinct list of major holidays and possible promotions that is a great tool to get you thinking about how to use holidays in your marketing throughout the year. So, here it is …

Jan: New Year's

Ideas: "New Year's - New You/New Start," "Get rid of last year's inventory"

Feb: Valentine's Day

Ideas: "Give yourself the _____ you'll love," "We love you and want to do something special for you"

Feb: Mardi Gras

Idea: Mardi Gras theme promotion

Feb: Chinese New Year

Idea: Year of the rooster "Wake up your __
___financial genius_____"

Feb: Groundhog Day

Idea: "You'll get an extra 6 weeks to pay because the groundhog saw his shadow"

March: St. Patrick's Day

Ideas: "Make Your Friends Green with Envy with _____" "Your lucky day"

March: Spring Break

Ideas: Spring break savings, getaway contest

April: April Fool's Day

Idea: "These discounts are so low my accountant thought this was an April Fool's Day joke"

April: Tax Day

Idea: "I need to pay for my taxes"

May: Mother's Day

Idea: "Mother always said you should _____"

June: Father's Day/Graduation

Idea: "Graduate to a new _____"

July: 4th of July

Ideas: "Watch fireworks explode when you _____", "Celebrate your independence _____"

August: Back to school

Idea: "Kids aren't the only ones that can get a new look for back to school"

Sept: Fall

Ideas: "Fall Special," "Harvesting Big Savings"

October: Halloween

Idea: "Give yourself a treat this month"

November: Election Day

Idea: "Elect a new _____"

November: Thanksgiving

Idea: "Thank you to our best customers"

Dec: Holidays

Idea: "Happy Holidays - winter sale," "Ho ho ho – Can't beat the fat man so we're having a sale"

example #1 – valentine's day taj mahal postcard

Connecting a story with a holiday is one of my favorite OUTRAGEOUS techniques.

And so one year at my menswear store, I connected Valentine's Day to the greatest gift of love ever given. That's right, I claimed the Taj Mahal as an OUTRAGEOUS gimmick.

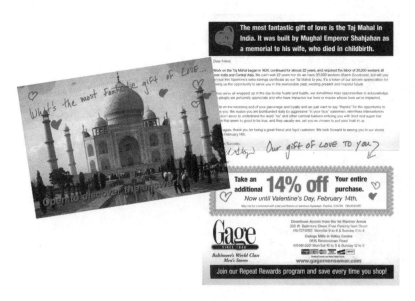

Gage Menswear Valentine's postcard front and inside. You can see this in full color when you claim your FREE CD of all of the exhibits in this book by using the form on page 312.

And there it is, in handwriting surrounded by hand-drawn hearts— "What's the most fantastic gift of love… [and at the bottom] Open to discover the answer!"

And behind it, as you see, is a photo of the Taj Mahal.

And so, of course, you open to discover the answer is …

The most fantastic gift of love ever given was the Taj Mahal, and, as you see, the inside of the card goes on to tell the story of why it was built, and then in a quick "reason why" twist, I explain how my sincere appreciation is my Taj Mahal gift.

And, tying the theme of love into Valentine's Day, the coupon is, of course, for 14 percent off.

The essential elements are there, including the offer and deadline, and at the bottom, as expected, is the pertinent information of location, store hours, phone number, etc.

example #2 - ben glass's 4th of july wallet mailing

How cool would it be to go to a Fourth of July party and pull out a flag wallet to show your friends and family?

Pretty cool!

And Ben Glass, a lawyer who helps other lawyers with marketing (www. greatlegalmarketing.com), knew this. So one year in late June, while trying to reach some unconverted leads, he sent out exactly that—a flag wallet with a sales letter headlined "Effective, Ethical and Outside The Box Marketing For Personal Injury Attorneys."

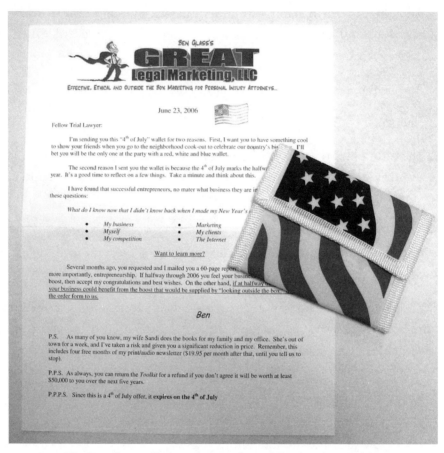

Ben Glass's wallet mailing. *You can see this in full color when you claim your FREE CD of all of the exhibits in this book by using the form on page 312.*

I, at first, can't get past the headline without thinking he missed an opportunity for a lawyer joke. But that's just my way of drawing attention to the elephant in the room, and besides, all lawyers know all the good lawyer jokes anyway.

But that is a minor difference of opinion on approach. The rest of the campaign is brilliant. It ties the holiday to the gift, which is memorable and will most likely be used, and the letter itself even has a little flag at the top.

Obviously a flag wallet on the Fourth of July is fun, and it's memorable! Once again, he's entering the conversation going on in the person's head with the approaching holiday.

OUTRAGEOUS boost

Unconverted leads are those people who have requested information from you in the past but have not yet purchased. A holiday is a great time to reach out to these people again because it gives you a "reason why." One of the things that Dan Kennedy always teaches is there is money to be gotten from people who have expressed interest in the past but have not bought yet.

example #3 - yanik silver's halloween campaign

A few Halloweens ago, Yanik Silver was about to release his "Ultimate At Home Internet Copywriting Course" when he decided to take advantage of the holiday.

Halloween may be the easiest holiday to have fun with, and Yanik Silver is a master. Yanik first remembered that he had been to a Halloween party the previous year and had dressed as "The Count" from Sesame Street.

So he had a photo. All he needed was a campaign to go with it.

The first thing he did was send out a short eight-line e-mail from "Count Yanik" to his customer list. He then directed his readers to a Web site for a "terrifyingly profitable message."

And that's when his message became really fun.

His Web site had Flash animation with an animated bat that turned into Count Yanik, using his real voice to relay his message.

OUTRAGEOUS resource

For flash animation at a reasonable price, see www. rentacoder.com.

Yanik Silver's online Halloween promotion.
You can see this in full color when you claim your FREE CD of all of the exhibits in this book by using the form on page 312.

At that page, as you can see, is another link to a PDF preview, keeping the customer engaged.

And then Yanik continues his Halloween-themed campaign in a step-by-step process until you almost can't wait to see what he's going to do next.

Of course, in his regular e-mail communications he uses phrases like "monster wealth" and "frightening profits," but he continues to have fun with the holiday theme later in a more elaborate Web landing page with his sales letter "written" in blood—or rather, a dripping bloody font.

Hurry! Only ~~77~~ 72 Discounted Packages Available

"OOPS"
You missed out on my Ultimate Internet
Copywriting Workshop – Don't miss out TWICE!

It's Spooky! You're Exactly One Ad, Web Site or Sales Letter Away From a Terrifying Fortune When You...

"DISCOVER HOW TO MASTER THE SHOCKINGLY SCARY SKILL THAT POURS MONEY INTO YOUR BANK ACCOUNT DAY & NIGHT..ALMOST LIKE MAGIC!"

Here's The Secret Formula For Creating More *Ghastly* Sales,
More *Frightening* Profits, More *Monster* Wealth &
More of ANYTHING Else You Could Ever Want...
Using Nothing More Than Your Keyboard or a Pen

 Listen to an audio message from
Yanik "The Count" Silver

Yanik Silver's landing page for his ONLINE Halloween promotion.
You can see this in full color when you claim your FREE CD
of all of the exhibits in this book by using the form on page 312.

As you notice, there is also an audio message from "The Count" and a continuing use of the Halloween theme.

It just shouts out, "Fun! ... OUTRAGEOUS FUN!!"

And Yanik goes on to present a Frankenstein image, a boiling cauldron, and even a bat next to the sentence "Am I batty?"

But he still wasn't finished as he continued with a follow-up e-mail that contained a link to another audio message from "The Count."

And Yanik says this campaign sold 114 packages of his material for $114,350—pretty good for one holiday campaign!

example #4 - the count glazula glazer-kennedy halloween promotion

I can "Count" too!

And so I did when Dan Kennedy sent out an e-mail letter with the subject: "This is Frightening!"

In Dan's letter, he told the story of how I wanted to lower prices for our Glazer-Kennedy products and how he was scared that the prices were too low, and then the reader was directed to a Web site where I was dressed as Count Glazula.

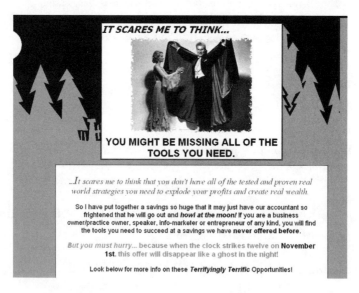

Glazer-Kennedy Insider's Circle "Count Glazula" Online Promotion.
You can see this in full color when you claim your FREE CD
of all of the exhibits in this book by using the form on page 312.

This was an OUTRAGEOUSLY successful Halloween campaign, proving the power of "The Count" in marketing.

But what it really proves again is that holidays offer a great "reason why" to hold a campaign. And, they also offer you an opportunity to have fun!

example #5 - royalty rewards program by rory fatt

Rory Fatt is the top marketing consultant to the restaurant industry in the world, and I've worked with him to develop an outstanding loyalty program for many categories of businesses including restaurants, retailers, and auto repair shops, which is called Royalty Rewards.

Royalty Rewards is a swipe card program that allows customers to accumulate points from purchases and then to redeem those points with gift certificates that they can use at their businesses.

Frankly, I believe that EVERY business should have some form of loyalty program because it works! For example, those businesses who use Royalty Rewards find that their customers return much more often and spend more each year. How could you ask for more?

Rory's original idea was to teach businesses to do this for themselves. But he found they'd rather have it done for them, and now he has nearly 1,000 businesses with more than 3 million customers enrolled in the program.

But the program is more than just a loyalty program. It also is a marketing program because everyone who is in the program is on a list. And that list includes great information including purchase history.

Rory then took the program a step further by creating holiday-themed campaigns for customers enrolled in the program. Each campaign is different, but the idea is to marry holiday-themed campaigns to your customer loyalty program—called Royalty Rewards if you do business with us. Here is a collage of holiday-themed cards that Rory sends out for businesses in our program.

James Smith

Happy Half Birthday!

We've Checked Our Records and It's
Only Six Months Until Your Special Day
and We Want to Help You Celebrate!

Please accept this gift of a
FREE Dinner Valued to $10
to come back and see us.

 See back for offer details! ▶

Examples of Royalty Rewards trademark-protected holiday postcards
for Father's Day, Halloween, Valentine's Day, anniversaries, Mother's Day,
half anniversaries, birthdays, and half birthdays.

OUTRAGEOUS resource

If you would like to find out about the "best" loyalty program
that I know about where everything is practically "done for
you," go to www.Royaltyrewards.com/outrageous.

---

example #6 – b2b marketing using oddball holidays

In 2007, Glazer-Kennedy Insider's Circle held a Holiday Promotions Contest, and the winner was an orthodontist who was aiming to get referrals from general dentists' offices in his area.

This orthodontist's name is Dr. Brian Bergh, and he cleverly took advantage of oddball holidays such as National Pistachio Day and National Ice Cream Day to send gifts with a personal letter to dentists' offices (B2B/ peer-to-peer marketing).

The letter always included some bit of personal information, and then the gift was tied to the letter and the oddball holiday. It was brilliant.

Here, for instance, is the letter for National Pistachio Day.

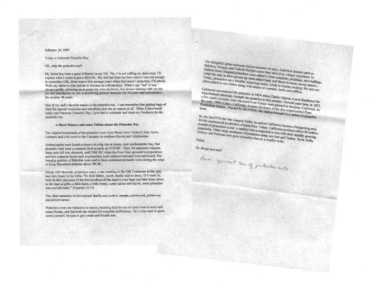

Dr. Brian Bergh's National Pistachio Day letter. You can see this in full color when you claim your FREE CD of all of the exhibits in this book by using the form on page 312.

This works brilliantly because he's reminding the dentists out there that he exists, and he is sending a gift.

It is so well written and so personal. The National Pistachio Day letter begins with a reference to his father, who loved pistachios, which makes it memorable on a different level and he comes across as the kind of person you would want to refer a patient to.

And by choosing the oddball holidays, he stands out from those using the common holidays that everyone is aware of.

For example, Dr. Bergh also used follow-up letters of other oddball holidays such as National Siblings Day, the birthday of Winnie the Pooh creator A.A. Milne, and National Ice Cream Day.

In the case of National Ice Cream Day, Dr. Bergh sent a gallon of ice cream along with a nice letter.

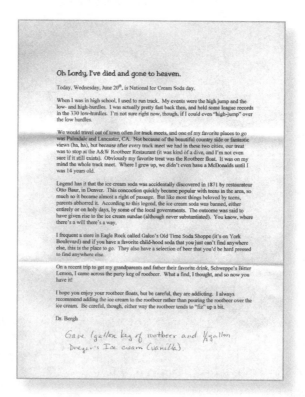

Dr. Brian Bergh's National Ice Cream Day letter. *You can see this in full color when you claim your FREE CD of all of the exhibits in this book by using the form on page 312.*

246

Here's the best news. By using oddball holidays and related gifts to stimulate referrals, Dr. Bergh's referrals went up 300 percent.

Three hundred percent!!!

example #7 – gage memorial day ad

So what happens on Memorial Day that you can take advantage of?

Gage Menswear Memorial Day newspaper ad. You can see this in full color when you claim your FREE CD of all of the exhibits in this book by using the form on page 312.

How about a cookout?

Well, that's exactly what we did at my menswear store one year when we asked, "What would we have to do this Memorial Day to get you to start the cookout after 5 p.m.?"

But we didn't just ask. We designed a catchy newspaper ad to look like a coupon and draw you in.

This ad features an eye-catching headline, a prominent deadline, and something else—a heavy-dashed border that gives the appearance of a coupon even though the ad is NOT a coupon. Americans love coupons, so your eyes naturally go to that dashed-line border and what's inside it.

OUTRAGEOUS **boost**

Putting "dashed" borders around display ads will increase readership even when you are not making a coupon offer.

example #8 – gage leap day ad

February 29 is special.

As I mentioned at the beginning of this chapter, once every four years, we get to leap, and so in my menswear business we used the special day as a chance to have a sale. It even gave us great "reason why" copy—we called it a rent-free day.

This was a really easy and fun promotion that only involved sending out an inexpensive 4 x 6 inch postcard.

We discovered that Leap Day is as good a day as any to hold a promotion. It's actually rather advantageous, but then tying a promotion to any holiday is advantageous if you can deliver the "reason why."

In fact, a member of one of my private coaching groups ran a seminar over a Leap Day and used the "rent free" ballroom theme as the reason why he could make the seminar registration fee lower. He got more sign-ups than ever before. As you can see, what works in one business is easily transferred to another when you put your mind to it.

Gage Menswear's front and back Leap Day postcard. You can see this in full color when you claim your FREE CD of all of the exhibits in this book by using the form on page 312.

Take a look around. Our Congress has created a holiday for every single date on the calendar, and a little imagination can make any of these days special, if you so desire.

OUTRAGEOUS resource

For a more detailed list of all holidays you can use for possible marketing campaigns, see Appendix B at the back of the book.

Sizzling Outrageous Summation

1) Holidays are already on people's minds, so enter the conversation in their minds and use the holidays to create OUTRAGEOUSLY successful advertising.

2) Businesses have anniversaries every year, and you should use them to hold a promotion because they are believable.

3) The top four holidays are Christmas, Halloween, Valentine's Day, and Mother's Day.

4) Tying a promotion to a holiday increases response.

5) Oddball holidays are attention-grabbing days.

12) Sampling Some Really OUTRAGEOUS Ideas

What if a gorilla wearing a gold bow tie, a gold vest, and a gold top hat brought you a package? Would you accept it and open it? Okay, let's say it was a courier wearing a gorilla suit, not a real gorilla. Would you accept it and open it then?

Kellene Bishop dispatched a coordinated set of such gorilla couriers one afternoon in Atlanta, proving that these techniques translate into all markets—even those that deal with people who deal with more affluent customers or with large transaction sizes.

Kellene, you see, arranges financing for multi-million-dollar commercial real estate purchases, and once she got into the business, she realized there was a huge opportunity for many people just like her.

She knew how to do it. So she started teaching classes—seminars really—on how to take advantage of the huge market, which is $1 trillion in commercial real estate that NEEDS to be refinanced in the next three years. It was a big, open market.

Kellene knew that she could teach smaller lenders how to think big and become big lenders and make big money in the process. That is, they'd make big money, and she'd make big money teaching them.

So she used a number of techniques to get her message out, but my favorite was one she used in Atlanta in 2006 when she sent out the gorillas.

She realized that the $1 trillion that needed to be refinanced was like an 800-pound gorilla in the room. Thus, the gorilla suits.

It actually turned into a bit of a publicity stunt that received free coverage in local media, bringing even more success to her promotion.

Of course, it wasn't easy. There was a lot of coordination that went into it, including acquiring the proper gifts for the gift boxes that the gorillas presented, getting the couriers to agree to wear gorilla suits in Atlanta's scorching hot weather, and handwriting an individual sales letter to each prospective client.

She was selling a $10,000 seminar and promising that if they followed her program they would earn at least $700,000. It was OUTRAGEOUS on all counts, and the gorilla certainly proved the point.

no limit to how OUTRAGEOUS you want to be?

OUTRAGEOUS doesn't mean offensive.

However, OUTRAGEOUS sometimes can be offensive to some. If you dare walk that line, just remember that it's a steep fall off of the wrong end. And yet, it certainly can draw attention.

Of course, it is important to know your audience and also their limits. This is not demographic rocket science. It is just ordinary smart guesswork— and using your good OUTRAGEOUS instinct for what's funny versus what's potentially offensive, and to whom.

Although you do need to be warned about being offensive, you need to equally and perhaps doubly be warned against being timid or boring. Your advertising NEEDS to be noticed ... remember, people are receiving thousands of advertising messages every week, and just about all of them are boring (and forgettable).

So, how OUTRAGEOUS do you want to be? Enough to GUARANTEE that you will be noticed!

OUTRAGEOUS ... OUTRAGEOUS ideas

No, that headline is not from the Department of Redundancy Department. It means that everything I teach is OUTRAGEOUS advertising, but some of those ideas are outrageous even in the realm of OUTRAGEOUS.

Some of them you've already seen in this book. For instance, in chapter 4, I described a few crazy mailers such as the coconut mailer and the garbage can mailer. Those were outrageous OUTRAGEOUS ideas.

Here are some more.

the wizmark interactive urinal communicator

There are certain places where you can get a captive audience.

I wrote in chapter 8 about an advertisement on the wall of a dentist's office directly in view of where a patient looks when he or she is being treated. That's a captive audience.

Another is a men's urinal. Yes, a men's urinal can be a good place to advertise. You wouldn't think of it, would you?

And yet, someone has figured out the whole "captive audience" thing and designed a urinal deodorizer that is, well, activated by fluid hitting it. And that "action" then triggers a flashing light or a message running across it.

Who would use such a thing? I know of an attorney who uses it to great success in bars where he advertises for DWI clients. I also know of a professional speaker who uses it at seminars to encourage attendees to come to his session.

253

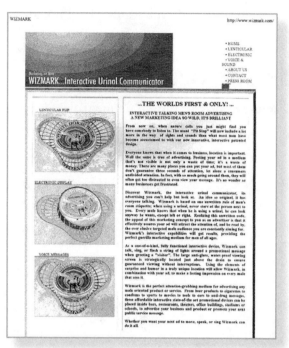

Wizmark Interactive Urinal Communicator. You can see this in full color when you claim your FREE CD of all of the exhibits in this book by using the form on page 312.

If you are a man, you might laugh when you're standing in front of a urinal, but you're not going anywhere until you finish what you came in to accomplish (said with political correctness).

Think about it! This is OUTRAGEOUS advertising that you will remember, which is the point of advertising. In fact, I'll bet that when you leave the men's room, you'll tell everyone else about the experience you just had and why all of the other males that are with you have to go and check it out.

OUTRAGEOUS resource

You can find information about Wizmark Interactive Urinals at www.wizmark.com.

And now, I'll change the subject. You're welcome.

the b2b "foot in the door" mailer

When you are in sales, especially in B2B sales, what are you trying to do? You are trying to get your "foot in the door." Right?

Well, of course you are.

So why not specifically say so?

In fact, why not just send a foot? You know ... to the door ... or in the mail.

No, really. Why not?

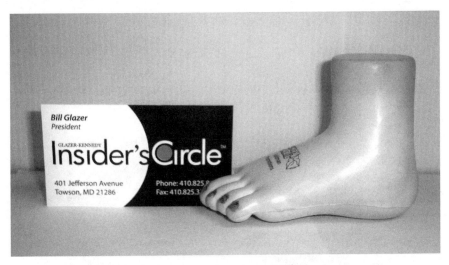

Foot In The Door Mailing. *You can see this in full color when you claim your FREE CD of all of the exhibits in this book by using the form on page 312.*

After all, one of the biggest struggles of all salespeople is simply getting in to see the decision maker. So, this campaign allows you to send a box in the mail that is opened up and accompanied by the foot with your business card wedged between two of the toes and a letter that begins, "You're probably wondering why I am sending you this rubber foot in the mail. Well, I'm trying to get 'my' foot in the door" to see you.

It's OUTRAGEOUS, and it works!

the payroll pro cruiser

I'm a big believer in looking for opportunities in your business where you can grab attention with OUTRAGEOUS advertising. For example, earlier in the book I wrote about how you can use pre-recorded testimonials on your "on-hold" message or how a dentist's office can place a sign in its operatories to promote new patient referrals.

Well, if you have a business where you have vehicles on the street that travel around a lot, why not place an OUTRAGEOUS sign on them to grab attention?

In fact, why not just drive a sign? They do it in NASCAR; why can't you?

That's what David Reckford thought, and so he paid to have his car wrapped in his logo to promote his business.

Payroll Pro wrapped vehicle. You can see this in full color when you claim your FREE CD of all of the exhibits in this book by using the form on page 312.

And now, whenever his vehicle parks to drop off a business's payroll or drives around town, it is an OUTRAGEOUS moving message. And best of all, once you have this down, it's like the Energizer Bunny … it keeps on working and working and working and working!!!!

the half-birthday campaign

We all know that birthdays are just about always observed, but how many people older than the age of nine celebrate half birthdays?

Not many, right?

And that's exactly why Dean Killingbeck decided to use that concept as an OUTRAGEOUS promotion. Killingbeck, as you may recall from chapter 9, is a master marketer who has used demographic and birthday lists to great advantage for the turnkey systems he has put in place for many businesses.

So he also took it a step further.

Once he saw the extraordinary success his clients had with using his turnkey mailings for birthdays, he realized he could get twice the results by also developing mailings for half birthdays. Of course, he does it in an OUTRAGEOUS manner.

After all, a half-birthday celebration for an adult is OUTRAGEOUS in itself. But what really made it special was the approach. There was half an envelope with half a letter.

Connecting the OUTRAGEOUS dots in an OUTRAGEOUS way made this campaign OUTRAGEOUSLY successful.

And inside the half envelope, there was of course a half letter from the business owner with the half-birthday offer.

Half Birthday Envelope.
You can see this in full color when you claim your FREE CD of all of the exhibits in this book by using the form on page 312.

Half Birthday Letter. *You can see this in full color when you claim your FREE CD of all of the exhibits in this book by using the form on page 312.*

OUTRAGEOUS resource

Dean Killingbeck's company, New Customers Now, offers a turnkey service to mail half-birthday mailings as a terrific strategy to attract existing customers/clients/patients or "new" customers to your business. You can contact his company at www.newcustomersnow.net.

scent mailing

Scratch and sniff?

How about scent and sell!!!

That's exactly what ScentiSphere has done. They have created dozens of different scents that your printer can add to anything you mail in order to add another sense to your mailing.

So you no longer just read it. Now you read and also smell it. Best of all, the possibilities are endless. Here's a partial list of the different scents you can add to your mailings:

Apple Pie	Latte
Asphalt	Marijuana
Banana	Lemon
Buttered Popcorn	Leather
Cherry	Mint
Chocolate	New Car Smell
Christmas Tree	Orchid
Clean Cotton	Peach
Coffee	Peppermint
Daisy	Pineapple
Dill Pickle	Red Licorice
Fireplace Smoke	Stinky Cheese

French Fries

Gingerbread

Grass

Green Apple

Suntan Lotion

Tulips

Vanilla

Watermelon

It's Roses for a "Scent."
Call us and we will send roses in a plain box to mend, to thank, to express sympathy, or any expression you may wish to send.

Call
316.555.9787
Roses for a "Scent"
(We may even save a marriage)

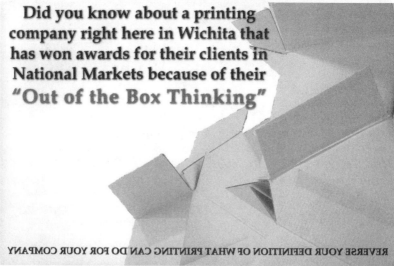

Did you know about a printing company right here in Wichita that has won awards for their clients in National Markets because of their "Out of the Box Thinking"

REVERSE YOUR DEFINITION OF WHAT PRINTING CAN DO FOR YOUR COMPANY

Scent Mailing Example. You can see this in full color when you claim your FREE CD of all of the exhibits in this book by using the form on page 312.

That's the idea of the scent mailing; it can send an actual aroma through the mail—aromas as diverse as the smell of a new car for an automobile dealership to the smell of marijuana for someone who sells plant food. Yes, that would be OUTRAGEOUS!

OUTRAGEOUS resource

You can find information about ScentiSphere at www. scentisphere.com.

your own postal stamp

The US Postal Service will now let you put almost any image you want on a stamp. You've probably seen Elvis and all the celebrities, but one of our Glazer-Kennedy Insider's Circle members, Bob Battle, an attorney, sent out a mailing with his own face on the stamp and above it the slogan, "In Bob We Trust."

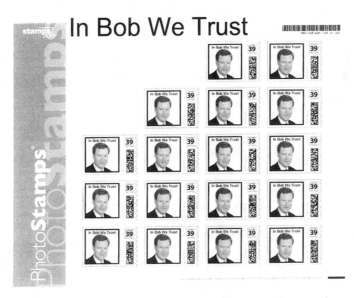

Bob Battle's postage stamp. You can see this in full color when you claim your FREE CD of all of the exhibits in the book by using the form on page 312.

Obviously this is a very smart way to increase the open rate of your mailings when the recipients are already familiar with you. They're going to say, "What is your picture doing on the stamp? I've just gotta open this up and find out what this is all about."

OUTRAGEOUS resource

You can find information about customized stamps at photo.stamps.com.

fortune cookie

Here is an OUTRAGEOUS idea: advertise inside of food.

That's what you can do if you try the fortune cookie advertisement. There are a lot of uses for this as you can print anything you want on the message inside of the fortune cookie.

For example, at my menswear stores I once ran a promotion where I sent out a postcard with a picture of a fortune cookie on it and told my customers to bring in the postcard to redeem it for a fortune cookie to discover how they could save a fortune with the discount inside the cookie when they opened it up.

These are really fun to do because as the casinos have taught us ... just about everybody loves "games of chance."

The Gage Fortune Cookie Postcard.
You can see this in full color when you claim
your FREE CD of all of the exhibits in this
book by using the form on page 312.

I've seen this fortune cookie approach applied to numerous businesses, typically with great success. In fact, in many cases an actual fortune cookie was delivered in the mail with headlines along the lines of:

"Here's The Secret To Making Your FORTUNE In _____"

"There a FORTUNE in Your Future"

"You Save A FORTUNE When You _____"

Sizzling Outrageous Summation

1) More OUTRAGEOUS gets more attention.

2) Know your audience; don't be offensive but never be boring.

3) You can advertise really OUTRAGEOUSLY in some really OUTRAGEOUS places.

4) You can be really OUTRAGEOUS without spending a lot of money by identifying opportunities you already have such as a message on hold, vehicles, signs, etc.

5) You can be really OUTRAGEOUS by using the senses of hearing, seeing, feeling, and even smelling.

13) Putting All The Pieces Together

Throughout this book, there have been a lot of lessons about how to do a number of different OUTRAGEOUS things and all the various elements that make them OUTRAGEOUSLY successful. They all work, but the truest and surest approach is to actually put it all together.

Every element, when put together, makes the sum greater than the parts.

There's a jewelry store in Daytona Beach, Florida, that knows all about this. The story of W.M. Ritzi & Co. Jewelers is a great example of OUTRAGEOUS growth from an OUTRAGEOUS and well-executed campaign.

This jewelry store launched a program to get Rolex repair business. According to a letter written to me from the owner, Cindi Ritzi, "My business is up over 30 percent this year, in a climate where most jewelry businesses, across the board, are way down. My Rolex repair solicitation, 5-step sequence, has generated over $35,000 in new business for repairs alone with a 37 percent response rate and a total cost to implement of $1,350."

She spent $1,350 and generated $35,000 in business.

OUTRAGEOUS!

Here's what she did—she used all the elements in chapters 5–9 of this book. She used a headline, offer, and deadline. She personalized her greeting and used graphics to enhance her message.

And what was her message? She was repairing Rolex watches at a fair price. She had testimonials. She sent a jumbo postcard. She sent a personalized #10 envelope. She sent a voice broadcast and finally a "follow-up" letter of regret. That's right, she was sequential.

And when all of the elements come together like this, the results are OUTRAGEOUSLY successful.

ONE ... the worst number in marketing

If you have one campaign that works in one particular media, don't mess with success. However ...

Just because you have one campaign that works in one particular media doesn't mean the world can't change in an instant. It can and will, and you'd better be ready. After the fact is too late.

Therefore, the worst number in marketing is "ONE." There is simply too much risk involved with throwing everything you have into one media.

Instead, the advice here is the same as any good financial advice ... diversify.

diversity leads to stability

For example, I work with a guy who was having great success advertising in his local market on a particular radio program hosted by a particular radio host. This host had helped this business grow greatly when he advertised my client's business, but when I suggested that the business needed more than one media to get its message out, the owner said he was doing just fine with the radio personality's sixty-second spots.

Well, one day the radio host landed a new job in another market. Good for the radio host ... not so good for the business owner.

And that's the problem. It's very seductive for an entrepreneur to fall prey to success and ignore stability.

OUTRAGEOUS exercise

Here is a list of twenty different media. Check off those you are using. Try to devise ways you could use the other media to make them part of an overall campaign.

- Newspaper ads
- Magazine ads
- Free standing inserts
- Radio
- Web sites
- E-mails
- Door hangers
- Postcards
- Publicity
- Self mailers

- Billboards
- Exterior signs
- Interior signs
- TV
- Voice broadcast
- Telemarketing
- Sales letters
- Advertorials
- Referral marketing
- Online banner ads

Perhaps the most seductive of all current media is the Internet. And that's really all the Internet is—a form of media. Sure, it's still new and seductive to use. But it's not so different than any other media. It's one option. But it's not the only option, and you can be very vulnerable if it is the ONLY form of media you use.

In fact, there is no "only option." Instead, the best option to guarantee success is to diversify and get your message across in many different media. By having several different things going on, you increase your exposure across a broad spectrum of customer media habits.

And the best part about stability under this program of OUTRAGEOUS advertising is that, by design, diversity leads to more than stability—it leads to more success as the cumulative message gets heard in different ways.

One final advantage of diversity is your ability to gauge results in many different media so you actually find out what works instead of simply guessing and hoping. This then gives you the confidence to spend more money on campaigns and media that work.

realizing the business you're in

Are you ready to make a real leap in sales and profits?

Then it's time to realize the real business that you are in, which is different than the sign you hang above your door. Success means shifting the paradigm so that you think in terms of being a marketer for your business. That, truly, is your business.

And so a professional dedicated approach to marketing your business and learning everything you can to market it better is the proper response to this new realization. Even with my experience, I attend at least two seminars a year just to keep myself engaged and learning. I am always on the lookout for new ideas. The marketing guru Zig Ziglar calls this "sharpening your axe," meaning that in order to be very productive at chopping down trees, you have to constantly keep a sharp axe instead of allowing the one you have to go dull. The same applies with constantly being a student of marketing. I find this process incredibly useful.

And hopefully, by now, you realize how important this paradigm shift is to your future success. Think like a marketer because marketing is your job. Without it, all your other jobs would disappear.

And by thinking like a marketer, you will find diverse paths to the same goal of sales. In fact, diversity is your friend and ally, and knowledge is your weapon, and a multi-tiered campaign is always your best option.

the bob davidson ford campaign

When the Bob Davidson Ford dealership in Baltimore, Maryland, purchased another local dealership and merged the two, they wanted to get the word out to customers—especially of the dealership that was being acquired.

So the first OUTRAGEOUS step taken was to send a sales letter out in an oversized (9 x 12) envelope labeled "Rush Priority Express."

Bob Davidson Ford/Lincoln/Mercury Rush Priority Express Envelope.
You can see this in full color when you claim your FREE CD
of all of the exhibits in this book by using the form on page 312.

This envelope is an example of something delivered in the mail looking important and demanding attention. When you receive something that says, "Rush Priority Express," you have to open it.

OUTRAGEOUS resource

"Rush Priority Express" envelopes are available through Handy Mailing Service. You can contact them by phone at (316) 944-6258.

And inside, the dealer sent a three-page sales letter announcing the merger and some deals. The first thing you notice, of course, is the headline, and then you see another trick you've learned earlier in this book—personalization. That's right, this letter is addressed to a specific name.

And so it begins to fit together. But wait, there's more!

And that is the point of putting it all together—giving more. In the letter itself are offers and deadlines and graphics and double readership and multiple aspects to the message. But wait, there's more!

The letter also included three separate coupons for different discounts on service at the dealership.

OUTRAGEOUS boost

The more individual items that are in a piece of mail, the better the response because it keeps the reader involved for longer.

And so the campaign with its mailing was very successful. But wait, there's more!

After the initial mailing campaign, the dealership then sent out a voice broadcast to the customers of the old dealer and announced the exact information in the three coupons. This extra step really pushed things forward.

bob davidson ford/lincoln/mercury voice broadcast script:

Hi, this is Fred Onnen from Towson Ford just following up on a letter I sent you about THE MOST IMPORTANT MESSAGE I HAVE EVER SENT OUR CUSTOMERS IN THE PAST SIXTY YEARS.

Frankly, I've been swamped with phone calls, so I thought I'd try to contact our valued customers to clear up any confusion. I decided to merge our market area with Bob Davidson Ford, which now provides you with an experience like never witnessed before in the Baltimore area. Now when you patronize Bob Davidson Ford at 1845 E. Joppa Road, you will experience The ULTIMATE Ford Store.

This is just a reminder that the three great gift certificates I sent you expire this Monday, March 12th, and one of them is good for a FREE oil and filter change. If you can't find your certificates, that's no problem. Just go into the Service Department at Bob Davidson Ford and tell them that Fred from Towson Ford sent you.

Thanks so much for your previous support and enjoy The ULTIMATE Ford Store at Bob Davidson Ford.

By the way ... if you have any questions, give Bob Davidson Ford a call at 410-823-3131.

The campaign, in fact, was so successful that they wished they had sent out only half the list and then followed up with the other half later because the shop literally became too busy to keep up.

the infusion software campaign

Infusion Software is a company that produces a customer relationship software (CRM) product that helps companies keep track of customers and their marketing campaigns.

It is a rather sophisticated, but affordable, software that makes it easy for companies to track results and make sure the steps in campaigns go out when they are designated to do so.

When Infusion wanted to market an optimization information kit for their Infusion CRM software, the company wanted to get the word out to existing customers in a fun yet deliberate way.

So, Infusion launched a nine-step campaign to sell their Marketing Excellence Kit. **Yes, nine steps.**

The company took advantage of a scenario involving some of their customers, who were actually Ultimate Fighting coaches, martial arts coaches, and wrestling coaches … "a group of folks you don't want to mess around with," claimed part of the Infusion marketing team.

It worked like this: These Ultimate Fighters attended a live customer event on optimizing the use of the software. Then the company sold DVDs of the seminar along with the manual from the event as its Marketing Excellence Kit. The campaign was based on the concept that the Ultimate Fighters didn't want Infusion giving their secrets away.

It started with a three-page e-mail describing the seminar and how optimizing the software with "insider secrets" would make profits skyrocket.

Following the e-mail came a fax, then another e-mail, and then another fax. Five e-mails, three faxes, and finally a letter was sent in the sequence.

Each step in this nine-step approach to existing customers then funneled readers to an online sales page, and it was focused on all customers who had not yet purchased the kit.

Here is a capsule look at their campaign.

Step	Media Type	Subject	Drive To...
1	E-mail #1	Leverage Infusion CRM to the hilt	Online Sales Page/Order (infusionsoft.com/me)
2	Fax #1	This man's fate is in YOUR hands...!	Online Sales Page/Order (infusionsoft.com/me)
3	E-mail #2	Infusion CRM Power Users Share Their Secrets	Online Sales Page/Order (infusionsoft.com/me)
4	Fax #2	This is YOUR last chance!	Online Sales Page/Order (infusionsoft.com/me)
5	E-mail #3	From the desk...Err... Hospital Bed of Clate Mask!	Online Sales Page/Order (infusionsoft.com/me)
6	Fax #3	The Phoenix Customer Relationship Trauma Center	Online Sales Page/Order (infusionsoft.com/me)
7	E-mail #4	URGENT: Time is RUNNING OUT...	Order through single click from e-mail
8	E-mail #5	A Big Fat 'Sorry' from Clate Mask!	Order through single click from e-mail
9	Letter	"Congratulations... and an apology!" Study/use the kit – reinforce the benefits	Study/use the kit— reinforce the benefits

Results: 141 orders ($210,000) and a bunch of interest around our next customer event.

Reported interesting results back from Infusion after the promotion was completed:

- We used our own software to manage and automatically execute the entire campaign and orders.

- Steps 1–6 generated **41%** of the orders and ran over a period of **58 days**.

- Steps 7 and 8 generated **59%** of the orders and ran over a period of **9 days**.

- Steps 7 and 8 employed a new CRM feature allowing our existing customers to order by simply clicking a link in an e-mail. When we removed barriers to ordering, our sales skyrocketed.

- Feedback on the campaign was very positive: customers liked seeing we enjoy having fun (not just a bunch of software nerds), they got a kick out of the cartoons, and it generated a lot of interest in our next customer event.

OUTRAGEOUS resource

The InfusionSoft COMPLETE nine-step campaign can be seen in full color when you claim your FREE CD of all of the exhibits in this book by using the form on page 312, but for now let me tell you about some of the highlights.

When you look at the campaign on the FREE CD, you'll notice that it all fits together. First of all, you'll notice that there actually is a flow to the campaign filled with personality. It's, in fact, a bit of a story … an OUTRAGEOUS story.

And the story keeps people engaged. Even if they don't buy after the first steps, the story gains power with each retelling and tweaking of the general idea that these Ultimate Fighters were upset with the owner of the company for giving away their "insider secrets."

It's funny and it's fun—and best of all, it's memorable because it is OUTRAGEOUS.

The first letter simply introduces the product and the story behind it—including the Ultimate Fighters.

The next correspondence in the sequence is a fax that shows a fun image of the president of Infusion, Clate Mask, being held in a headlock.

And, as in each correspondence, this has all the essential elements of a great ad including a headline, an OUTRAGEOUS image, personalization, an offer, and a deadline. And it connects and refers back to the previous correspondence.

A lot of why this works is because of the personality that Clate Mask displays in his correspondence—a fun, funny pitch that keeps the reader reading.

In e-mail number three, the fifth correspondence, Clate pretends to be writing from a hospital bed because one of the Ultimate Fighters hurt his neck. In it, he tells of his fanatic interest in getting the information out. It's funny, and it keeps the interest. Check it out.

As the campaign wears down, on the seventh and eighth correspondences, Clate pushes the concept of a deadline and a great opportunity flying by. And, as you can see in the chart about the campaign, those last two there-really-is-a-deadline pieces generated 59 percent of all the orders in just nine days.

Finally, the last correspondence is sent to customers who agreed to try the material on a trial basis and then purchase. It is a letter of thanks with many reinforcements of the benefits of the kit.

This letter, with a clever apology for sending this decide-now material during the busy Christmas season, comes with the trial material.

The subject moves completely away from the Ultimate Fighter theme and into a cheery Christmas theme with the promise of lots of profits. This final, personalized reinforcement is a nice touch, showing involvement to the end.

I also want to point out that this campaign didn't use just one media. NO! This is a combination of three different diverse media:

1) E-mail

2) Fax

3) Snail mail

After all, "diversity leads to Stability" even when you are a software provider that delivers everything online.

OUTRAGEOUS resource

Information about InfusionSoft can be found at http://infusionsoft.com/outrageous.

the glazer-kennedy super conference campaign

YES, I practice what I preach.

So when Dan Kennedy and I set out to promote our 2008 MARKETING & MONEY-MAKING SuperConference in Nashville, Tennessee—featuring Gene Simmons of the rock band KISS—we put all of these lessons into practice. The seminar also featured George Ross, who is Donald Trump's vice president and often seen on the hit TV show The Apprentice, as well as the president of High Point University and chairman of the board of The Great Harvest Bread Company, Nido Quebin.

Since we wanted to make this our highest attended SuperConference ever, we were methodical and yet OUTRAGEOUS in our approach. Oh … and we were also relentless.

a three-phase campaign

The SuperConference campaign is built in phases.

Phase one is for the first early bird discount, which begins in November and ends December 31.

Once we see where we are with registrations, we then have a strategy meeting to schedule out phase two, which includes some breakout campaigns such as one to new members and another one to long-time members who have never been to a SuperConference before.

Then we move to phase three, which is again to see where we are with registrations and then decide what we need to do from there.

PHASE 1

Starting in mid-November, we sent out a big mailing to our members announcing the details of the SuperConference. This was a very elaborate mailing that actually went out in a UPS envelope that was sent through the U.S. Postal Service. You wouldn't believe how many of our Glazer-Kennedy Insider's Circle members asked us how we were able to send out a UPS envelope through a U.S. post office. This certainly put us in their A pile!

The Glazer-Kennedy Insider's Circle UPS envelope. You can see this in full color when you claim your FREE CD of all of the exhibits in this book by using the form on page 312.

OUTRAGEOUS resource

RST Marketing has the exclusive contract to mail UPS envelopes through the U.S. Postal Service. You can find details about them at http://rstmkt.com/.

As I mentioned above, inside this envelope was a very elaborate mailing comprising twenty-eight pages explaining everything about the SuperConference.

***COVER** of the Glazer-Kennedy Insider's Circle SuperConference*
twenty-eight-page mailing. *You can see this in full color when you claim your*
FREE CD of all of the exhibits in this book by using the form on page 312.

But we didn't just stop with the twenty-eight-page letter. Inside the letter was another letter with a SuperConference keychain that promoted the fact that we were giving away a brand-new Ford Mustang convertible at the SuperConference.

A plastic bag was the first thing you saw when you opened the envelope, and the bag contained a key ring with our SuperConference logo on it—looking much like the Superman logo—and a card asking, "May I give you the keys?"

And then inside was a photo of a beautiful red Ford Mustang convertible asking the same question.

SuperConference Ford Mustang giveaway insert. You can see this in full color when you claim your FREE CD of all of the exhibits in this book by using the form on page 312.

And also included was a letter explaining the Mustang giveaway and introducing the seminar, its benefits, and the deadline for the fast-filling event.

The campaign had begun, and we received great response to our first mailing. But we were not going to stop at just one attempt to get people to come to our great seminar.

Instead, we just went more OUTRAGEOUS.

Beginning on December 10 at 6 a.m., we began sending out e-mails to our top-level Gold-Club members talking about our upcoming seminar and our December 31 deadline to register and get an "Early Bird Discount" of $500.

And in that initial e-mail, a KISS was given. The e-mail, which came from Dan Kennedy, talked extensively about this "real life superhero," Gene Simmons, coming to our seminar to give business-building information. This genius who owns all the licensing rights to the KISS brand was easy to sell as a featured speaker.

It was a great introduction, but it was only the beginning. Talk about putting it all together. This campaign was put all together.

Between December 10 and our early bird deadline of December 31, we sent eighteen e-mails. Each was extensive and detailed a continuation on our message that we were selling out quick and this was the opportunity of a lifetime.

Putting eighteen of these e-mails in here might be overkill, although let's face it, it would be OUTRAGEOUS! Instead, here is an example of one of these e-mails.

EMAIL #18 Sunday, December 30ᵗʰ (6am)

From: Lois Lane (info@dankennedy.com)
Sent:
To:
Subject: Last Chance. Final Notice

LAST CHANCE. FINAL NOTICE.

Dear (First Name),

****
You've got to see Greg Woodley's Comments about why he traveled 33-hours from Australia to attend The SuperConference: Click Here:

****

THERE ARE ONLY 24 HRS LEFT TO CLAIM THE FREE BONUS DAY EXCLUSIVELY WITH DAN KENNEDY.

Lois Lane here....Ace Reporter for THE DAILY PLANET with a....

NEWS FLASH: NEARLY 800 KENNEDYIZED ENTREPRENEURS AND MARKETERS GATHER WITH THE 2008 LEAGUE OF EXTRAORDINARY EXPERTS, AND SUPERSTAR SPEAKERS FOR THREE DAYS OF EXCHANGING MONEYMAKING SECRETS SO EARTHSHAKINGLY POWERFUL IT ROCKS METROPOLIS WITH GREATER FORCE THAN THE ASTEROID SHOWER OF 1998.....

And YOU are about to MISS IT.....cowering like that chicken Clark Kent under your covers at home instead of mixing it up with the movers 'n shakers of the marketing world!

Is that really what you want for yourself?....do you want to be a meek and mild-mannered ordinary business owner or a Super-Entrepreneur in possession of SUPER MARKETING & MONEY-MAKING Marketing Powers unlike any mere mortal can imagine....and a Super bank account to match?

Make the right choice.....register online at www.dankennedyssl.com/Super2008   before DECEMBER 31ˢᵗ at midnight Metropolis time, and you'll get your LAST CHANCE to receive a $500.00 EARLY BIRD DISCOUNT.

Your Reporter For Life,

Lois

PS: What would a SUPER-Conference be without a SUPER-GUARANTEE?

Guarantee: If, at the dinner break of Day#1, you do NOT agree that you are participating in a Life-Altering Event and Experience of SUPER Importance and Value to you, you may advise us of your disappointment, exit the Conference (and the Hotel), with a FULL, 100% REFUND OF YOUR FEE plus up to $500.00 REIMBURSEMENT of documented Air Travel and Hotel Costs.

www.dankennedyssl.com/Super2008

So, eighteen e-mails in twenty days is a lot, huh?

Well wait, there's more!

In addition to the e-mails, as the deadline approached, two faxes and one voice mail were sent out from "The Riddler" wondering why the person was late registering.

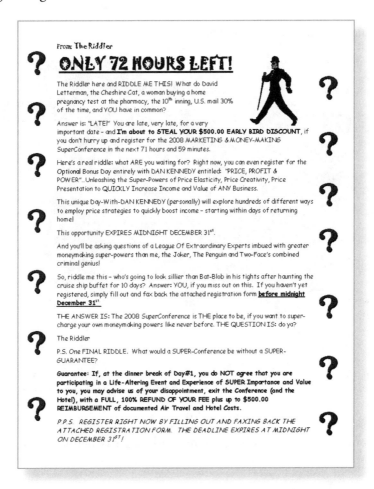

The Riddler fax sent out to Glazer-Kennedy Insider's Circle members.

Of course, a running theme throughout all of this initial campaign was that we were filling up fast and we could very well sell out at any moment.

Then we were even more OUTRAGEOUS. Since we were inviting the founder of the rock band KISS to speak at our conference, we had our Graphic Department photoshop Dan Kennedy, Peak Performance Coach Lee Milteer, and myself dressed up in something resembling a KISS rock band look and sent it out as an OUTRAGEOUS holiday greeting card.

The No B.S. Band holiday greeting card. You can see this in full color when you claim your FREE CD of all of the exhibits in this book by using the form on page 312.

And then the insert in that mailing told our members again about the SuperConference and discounts offered and all the benefits and, of course ... the deadline.

But then the deadline passed. So we had our strategy meeting and went on to ...

PHASE 2

We really did put it all together after we saw the results of phase one (which were spectacular). Of course, at Glazer-Kennedy, we already had some pieces in place that would help us immensely. For one, we have a monthly newsletter with over 20,000 subscribers.

So for our next three monthly newsletters we included an insert advertising our SuperConference to our members.

SuperConference newsletter inserts. You can see this in full color when you claim your FREE CD of all of the exhibits in this book by using the form on page 312.

Next, we segmented our list and found 700 names of people who had attended our SuperConference in previous years but, for whatever reason, had not yet signed up for the 2008 seminar.

This mailing went out in an envelope with two Superman Band-Aids on the envelope and the words "Your SuperConference Alumni protection is enclosed."

This specifically focused part of the bigger overall campaign generated twenty-three responses. It was effective for a number of reasons including, again, that even this step in the bigger campaign had all the essential elements and even some extra elements such as a grabber—in this case, Band-Aids all over the envelope and inside sales letter.

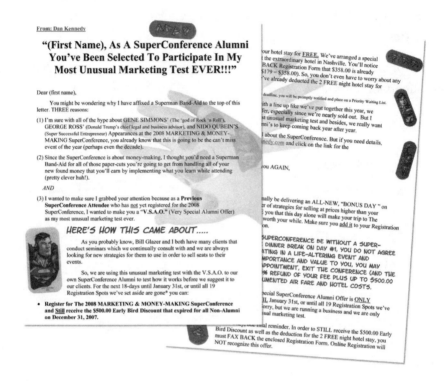

SuperConference Band-Aid mailing to previous attendees. *You can see this in full color when you claim your FREE CD of all of the exhibits in this book by using the form on page 312.*

Next, as part of the "Member" offer we featured what we called a "Very Special Member Offer" with details of how to save money in a number of ways.

Next, I compared myself to a jackass.

Hey, opportunity knocked, and by now you know I'm willing to be OUTRAGEOUS.

Here's what happened. My wife and I had gone on vacation in Greece earlier in the year, and when we were there, we encountered a man offering donkey rides. Well, I didn't want to ride the donkey up the hill, but I saw a great opportunity to get my photograph taken atop the jackass.

So when this phase of the campaign started, the photo was a natural to add to my OUTRAGEOUS attention-getting approach.

With a photograph of me aboard a jackass in my arsenal, all we needed to do now was build an approach. And so I decided to publicly compare myself to a jackass, proving again the old adage that the best humor is self-deprecating humor.

And it was. It was funny. Therefore, it caught attention. Check it out below.

SuperConference jackass mailing. You can see this in full color when you claim your FREE CD of all of the exhibits in this book by using the form on page 312.

As you can see, the mailing included a red-stamped tease about a CD enclosed and $200 in savings as well. And then the copy was funny and attention-getting.

Also included was something that looked like a letter "written" by "the Jackass who gave Bill Glazer a ride." And the card, in the donkey's writing, explains how the reader would feel like a jackass if he or she didn't attend the SuperConference.

Throughout the copy, the donkey kept writing about the SuperConference and even explained that there was a free CD enclosed with a preview of all the speakers.

And by including that audio CD we raised the level of the campaign significantly by entering into another powerful media.

This audio CD was one of our most successful pieces in the entire campaign. This combination of mail and audio media struck a chord.

OUTRAGEOUS resource

Audio CD self mailers are available at City Print USA. Call Steve Harshbarger at 1-866-907-1222 or e-mail sales@ cityprintusa.com.

By now we were just at about the capacity the room would hold in Nashville (about 1,400 people), but we weren't giving up yet. We moved to ...

PHASE 3

We continued to remind our list with our final newsletter inserts and an e-mail to let them know that the final member discount was about to expire. We were prepared to do more marketing, but fortunately we didn't have to because we reached our capacity.

As you would expect, the SuperConference was a great event, and I hope someday I can personally meet you at one of them. I don't know anyone who ever leaves one of these withOUT dozens of money-making strategies to take home and apply immediately to his or her business. Besides, the networking opportunities with "like-minded" entrepreneurs are priceless!!

Photo Of A Glazer-Kennedy Marketing & Money-Making Superconference.

In addition, at every SuperConference I always like to show the latest OUTRAGEOUS advertising examples that I have come across since the previous year. Everyone who attends learns "in living color" what you have learned throughout this book ...

OUTRAGEOUS Advertising
Is Outrageously Successful!

Sizzling Outrageous Summation

1)   One is the worst number in marketing; use multiple steps and multiple media.

2)   The business you are in is really the marketing business, and once you accept that, you'll see your sales and income skyrocket.

3)   Creating a theme for a big campaign creates energy for that campaign.

4) Make yourself into a personality—and have fun with it.

5) It's not necessary to plan out a campaign from start to finish at the beginning. Often results dictate how complicated and elaborate your campaigns need to be.

OUTRAGEOUS
Appendix A:

the 100 greatest headlines ever written

This list was put together for one reason: to provide you with a single source of ideas for writing headlines.

The easiest way to come up with a good headline is to sit down and read a large number of successful headlines. The idea is NOT to steal someone else's words, but to use them as templates in order to write your own and also develop a sense of what elements make a good headline.

For example, headline #1 is: THE SECRET OF MAKING PEOPLE LIKE YOU

The template is: THE SECRET OF _____

Here's an example of how several industries could use this headline.

Mortgage Broker:

THE SECRET OF SAVING HUNDREDS OF DOLLARS EACH
    MONTH ON YOUR COSTLY MORTGAGE PAYMENT

Pizza Shop:

THE SECRET OF FEEDING YOUR ENTIRE FAMILY A DELICIOUS
    DINNER FOR LESS THAN FORTY BUCKS

Dental Office:

THE SECRET OF A PERFECT SMILE

I hope you get the idea how to use these and find the words on the following pages a creative inspiration.

the 100 greatest headlines ever written:

1. The Secret of Making People Like You

2. A Little Mistake That Cost a Farmer $3,000 a Year

3. Advice to Wives Whose Husbands Don't Save Money – By a Wife

4. The Child Who Won the Hearts of All

5. Are You Ever Tongue-Tied at a Party?

6. How a New Discovery Made a Plain Girl Beautiful

7. How to Win Friends and Influence People

8. The Last 2 Hours Are the Longest – And Those Are the 2 Hours You Save

9. Who Else Wants a Screen Star Figure?

10. Do You Make These Mistakes in English?

11. Why Some Foods "Explode" in Your Stomach

12. Hands That Look Lovelier in 24 Hours – Or Your Money Back

13. You Can Laugh at Money Worries – If You Follow This Simple Plan

14. Why Some People Almost Always Make Money in the Stock Market

15. When Doctors "Feel Rotten" This Is What They Do

16. It Seems Incredible That You Can Offer These Signed Original Etchings – For Only $5 Each

17. Five Familiar Skin Troubles – Which Do You Want to Overcome?

18. Which of These $2.50 to $5 Best Sellers Do You Want - For Only $1 Each?

19. Who Ever Heard of a Woman Losing Weight - And Enjoying 3 Delicious Meals at the Same Time?

20. How I Improved My Memory in One Evening

21. Discover the Fortune That Lies Hidden in Your Salary

22. Doctors Prove 2 Out of 3 Women Can Have More Beautiful Skin in 14 Days

23. How I Made a Fortune with a "Fool Idea"

24. How Often Do You Hear Yourself Saying: "No, I Haven't Read It; I've Been Meaning To!"

25. Thousands Have This Priceless Gift – But Never Discover It!

26. Whose Fault When Children Disobey?

27. How a "Fool Stunt" Made Me a Star Salesman

28. Have You These Symptoms of Nerve Exhaustion?

29. Guaranteed to Go Through Ice, Mud or Snow – Or We Pay the Tow!

30. Have You a "Worry" Stock?

31. How a New Kind of Clay Improved My Complexion in 30 Minutes

32. 161 New Ways to a Man's Heart – In This Fascinating Book for Cooks

33. Profits That Lie Hidden in Your Farm

34. Is the Life of a Child Worth $1 to You?

35. Everywhere Women Are Raving About This Amazing New Shampoo!

36. Do You Do Any of These Ten Embarrassing Things?

37. Six Types of Investor – Which Group Are You In?

38. How to Take Out Stains...Use (Product Name) and Follow These Easy Directions

39. Today...Add $10,000 to Your Estate – For The Price of a New Hat

40. Does Your Child Ever Embarrass You?

41.   Is Your Home Picture Poor?

42.   How to Give Your Children Extra Iron – These 3 Delicious Ways

43.   To People Who Want to Write – But Can't Get Started

44.   This Almost Magical Lamp Lights Highway Turns Before You Make Them

45.   The Crimes We Commit Against Our Stomachs

46.   The Man with the "Grasshopper Mind"

47.   They Laughed When I Sat Down at the Piano – But When I Started to Play!

48.   Throw Away Your Oars!

49.   How to Do Wonders with a Little Land!

50.   Who Else Wants Lighter Cake – In Half the Mixing Time?

51.   Little Leaks That Keep Men Poor

52.   Pierced by 301 Nails....Retains Full Air Pressure

53.   No More Backbreaking Garden Chores for Me – Yet Ours Is Now the Show Place of the Neighborhood!

54.   Often a Bridesmaid, Never a Bride

55.   How Much Is "Worker Tension" Costing Your Company?

56.   To Men Who Want to Quit Work Someday

57.   How to Plan Your House to Suit Yourself

58.   Buy No Desk – Until You've Seen This Sensation of the Business Show

59.   Call Back These Great Moments at the Opera

60.   "I Lost My Bulges...And Saved Money, Too"

61.   Why (Brand Name) Bulbs Give More Light This Year

62.   Right and Wrong Farming Methods – And Little Pointers That Will Increase Your Profits

63. New Cake Improver Gets You Compliments Galore!

64. Imagine Me...Holding an Audience Spellbound for 30 Minutes

65. This Is Marie Antoinette – Riding to Her Death

66. Did You Ever See a "Telegram" from Your Heart?

67. Now Any Auto Repair Job Can Be "Duck Soup" for You

68. New Shampoo Leaves Your Hair Smoother – Easier to Manage

69. It's A Shame for You Not to Make Good Money – When These Men Do It So Easily

70. You Never Saw Such Letters as Harry and I Got About Our Pears

71. Thousands Now Play Who Never Thought They Could

72. Great New Discovery Kills Kitchen Odors Quick! – Makes Indoor Air "Country Fresh"

73. Take This 1-Minute Test – Of an Amazing New Kind of Shaving Cream

74. Announcing...The New Edition of the Encyclopedia That Makes It Fun to Learn Things

75. Again She Orders... "A Chicken Salad, Please"

76. For the Woman Who Is Older than She Looks

77. Where You Can Go in a Good Used Car

78. Check the Kind of Body You Want

79. "You Kill That Story – Or I'll Run You Out of the State!"

80. Here's a Quick Way to Break Up a Cold

81. There's Another Woman Waiting for Every Man – And She's Too Smart to Have "Morning Mouth"

82. This Pen "Burps" Before It Drinks – But Never Afterwards!

83. If You Were Given $200,000 to Spend – Isn't This the Kind of (Type of Product, But Not Brand Name) You Would Build?

84. "Last Friday...Was I Scared! – My Boss Almost Fired Me!"

85. 76 Reasons Why It Would Have Paid You to Answer Our Ad a Few Months Ago

86. Suppose This Happened on Your Wedding Day!

87. Don't Let Athlete's Foot "Lay You Up"

88. Are They Being Promoted Right Over Your Head?

89. Are We a Nation of Lowbrows?

90. A Wonderful Two Years' Trip at Full Pay – But Only Men with Imagination Can Take It

91. What Everybody Ought to Know... About This Stock and Bond Business

92. Money-Saving Bargains from America's Diamond Discount House

93. Former Barber Earns $8,000 in 4 Months as a Real Estate Specialist

94. Free Book – Tells You 12 Secrets of Better Lawn Care

95. Greatest Gold Mine of Easy "Things to Make" Ever Crammed into One Big Book

96. $80,000 in Prizes! Help Us Find the Name for These New Kitchens

97. Now! Own Florida Land This Easy Way...$10 Down and $10 a Month

98. Take Any 3 of These Kitchen Appliances – For Only $8.95 (Values up to $15.45)

99. Save 20 Cents on Two Cans of Cranberry Sauce – Limited Offer

100. One Place Setting Free for Every Three You Buy!

OUTRAGEOUS
Appendix B:

holidays to inspire you

People really love holidays, and they're great to tie into your OUTRAGEOUS marketing to make it really fun! Below is a list of many of the most well-known and not-so-well-known holidays that you can use in your marketing.

Every time you're looking to send out a marketing message to your customers/clients/patients, look over the list below and determine if you can tie one of the holidays into your message. They'll love it and so will you when you see the OUTRAGEOUSLY successful results!

Holiday List:

January 1	New Year's Day
January 1	Paul Revere's birthday
January 1	Betsy Ross's birthday (designed first U.S. flag)
January 8	Elvis Presley's birthday
January 14	Benedict Arnold's birthday (traitor in American Revolutionary War)
January 15	National Hat Day

	January 17	Al Capone's birthday (notorious 1920s gangster)
	January 17	Mohammad Ali's birthday
	January 18	Peter Roget's birthday (author of Roget's Thesaurus)
	January 19	National Popcorn Day
	January 21	Martin Luther King, Jr. Day (third Monday of January, traditionally January 15)
	February 2	Groundhog Day
	February 3	Super Bowl Sunday (currently the first Sunday of February)
	February 5	Mardi Gras (Christian; moveable based on Easter)
	February 6	Ash Wednesday (Christian; moveable based on Easter)
	February 6	George Herman "Babe" Ruth's birthday
	February 6	Monopoly first went on sale in 1935
	February 11	Thomas Alva Edison's birthday (inventor of the light bulb)
	February 14	Valentine's Day
	February 14	Jimmy Hoffa's birthday
	February 18	Presidents' Day (officially Washington's Birthday; third Monday of February, traditionally February 22)
	February 29	Leap Day
	March 2	Theodore Seuss Geisel's birthday, "Dr. Seuss"
	March 3	Alexander Graham Bell's birthday (invented the telephone)

March 9	Employee Appreciation Day
March 16 Palm	Sunday (Christian; Sunday before Easter)
March 17	St. Patrick's Day
March 17	The rubber band was invented in 1845
March 19	Wyatt Earp's birthday (Wild West lawman)
March 20	Vernal Equinox (based on sun), Laylat Al-Qadr (Islamic; moveable, based on lunar calendar)
March 21	Good Friday (Christian; Friday before Easter)
March 23	Easter Sunday (Christian; moveable, Sunday after first full moon during spring)
March 24	Easter Monday (Christian; Monday after Easter)
March 26	Make Up Your Own Holiday Day
April 1	April Fool's Day
April 1	The dollar sign was invented by Oliver Pollack in 1778
April 8	Hank Aaron broke Babe Ruth's record in 1974
April 13	Thomas Jefferson's birthday (third US president (1801–1809))
April 15	Leonardo da Vinci's birthday (artist, sculptor, inventor)
April 20	First day of Passover (Jewish; moveable based on Jewish calendar)
April 21	Patriot's Day/Marathon Monday (New England and Wisconsin only; third Monday of April)

	April 21	Queen Elizabeth II's birthday (queen of England)
	April 22	Earth Day
	April 25	Arbor Day
	April 27	Last day of Passover (Jewish; moveable, based on Jewish calendar)
	May 1	May Day
	May 5	Cinco De Mayo (Mexican holiday often observed in US)
	May 8	The US post office was established in 1794
	May 9	Lost Sock Memorial Day
	May 11	Mother's Day (second Sunday of May), Pentecost Sunday (Christian; 49 days after Easter)
	May 12	Florence Nightingale's birthday (a pioneer in the field of nursing)
	May 12	Yogi Berra's birthday (baseball player, manager)
	May 13	Reggie Jackson becomes the first Major League ballplayer to strike out 2,000 times
	May 14	Star Wars Day (George Lucas' birthday)
	May 22	The Loch Ness Monster was first sighted on May 22, 1933
	May 23	Ken Jennings' birthday (Jeopardy record winner)
	May 26	Memorial Day (last Monday of May, traditionally May 30)
	May 29	John F. Kennedy's birthday (35th US president, assassinated in office (1960–1963))

	June 1	Marilyn Monroe's birthday
	June 14	Flag Day
	June 14	Donald Trump's birthday
	June 15	Father's Day (third Sunday of June)
	June 19	Lou Gehrig's birthday (baseball player)
	June 20	Summer Solstice (based on sun)
	June 20	Bob Vila's birthday (TV handyman)
	June 23	The US Secret Service was created
	June 26	Abner Doubleday's birthday (invented the game of baseball)
	July 4	Independence Day
	July 4	Ann Landers' birthday (advice columnist)
	July 5	P. T. Barnum's birthday (showman, circus founder)
	July 20	Neil Armstrong becomes the first man to walk on the moon in 1969
	July 20	National Tug-O-War Contest
	July 22	Alex Trebek's birthday (host of TV game show Jeopardy)
	July 24	Amelia Earhart's birthday (pioneer aviator)
	July 30	Arnold Schwarzenegger's birthday (weightlifter, actor, governor of California)
	July 31	J.K. Rowling's birthday (author of "Harry Potter" series)
	August 1	Francis Scott Key's birthday (author of the national anthem)
	August 5	Neil Armstrong's birthday (first to walk on the moon)

August 13	Left Hander's Day
August 24	Cal Ripken Jr.'s birthday (played in 2,643 consecutive baseball games)
August 26	Macaulay Culkin's birthday (actor, starred in "Home Alone" movies)
August 29	Michael Jackson's birthday
September 1	Labor Day (first Monday of September)
September 1	"Dr. Phil" McGraw's birthday (TV personality)
September 2	First day of Ramadan (Islamic; moveable based on lunar calendar)
September 11	Patriot Day
September 18	Lance Armstrong's birthday (six time Tour de France cycling champion)
September 19	National Talk Like a Pirate Day (unknown origin, but it is an official holiday)
September 30	Rosh Hashanah (Jewish; moveable, based on Jewish calendar)
October 2	Eid al-Fitr Day after the end of Ramadan (Islamic; moveable, based on lunar calendar)
October 9	Yom Kippur (Jewish; moveable, nine days after first day of Rosh Hashanah)
October 13	Columbus Day (second Monday of October, traditionally October 12)
October 14	First day of Sukkot (Jewish; moveable, fourteen days after Rosh Hashanah)
October 16	Noah Webster's birthday (compiled first American English dictionary)
October 17	Evel Knievel's birthday (motorcycle daredevil)

October 20	Last day of Sukkot (Jewish)
October 22	Simchat Torah (Jewish; moveable, twenty-two days after Rosh Hashanah)
October 28	Bill Gates's birthday (Microsoft executive, multi-multi-billionaire)
October 30	Mischief Night
October 31	Halloween
November 1	All Saints' Day
November 4	Election Day (Tuesday after the first Monday of November)
November 8	Bram Stoker's birthday (novelist, wrote horror novel Dracula)
November 11	Veterans Day
November 23	William "Billy the Kid" Bonney's birthday (Wild West outlaw)
November 26	Charles Schulz's birthday (cartoonist, created Peanuts)
November 27	Thanksgiving (fourth Thursday of November)
November 28	Black Friday (Friday after Thanksgiving Day)
November 30	Dick Clark's birthday (TV personality)
December 2	Charles Ringling's birthday (formed Ringling Bros. circus)
December 7	Pearl Harbor Remembrance Day
December 12	Bob Barker's birthday (TV game show host)
December 22	First day of Hanukkah (moveable, based on Jewish calendar)
December 24	Christmas Eve (Christian)
December 25	Christmas Day (Christian)
December 26	First day of Kwanzaa (Kwanzaa is celebrated until January 1)

	December 29	Last day of Hanukkah (moveable, based on Jewish Calendar)
	December 31	New Year's Eve

OUTRAGEOUS
Appendix C:

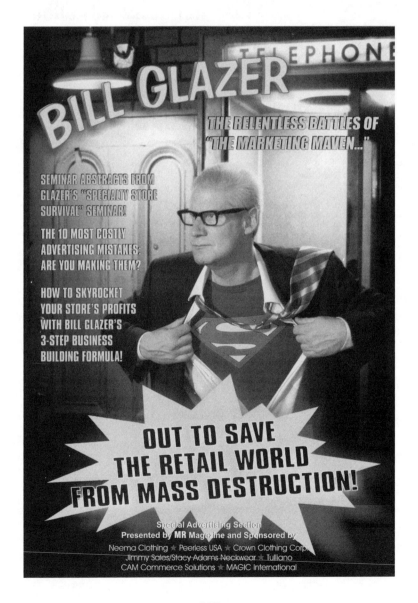

Bill Glazer: Successful Menswear retailer and creator of BGS Marketing, a System-oriented solution for retailers to cut the fat, waste and aggravation out of their marketing efforts.

HOW ONE RETAILER-TURNED-MARKETING-GURU IS DETERMINED TO HELP RETAILERS NOT JUST SURVIVE...BUT THRIVE!

An MR Las Vegas Seminar abstract

SPECIALTY STORE SURVIVAL:

Featuring Bill Glazer

WHO *IS* BILL GLAZER?

Perhaps you've read his "Marketing Maven" articles in MR Magazine...perhaps you've seen him speak at clothing shows...you may have even attended his most recent engagement at MAGIC in August where more than 240 profit-hungry men's and womens' clothing retailers came to soak up Glazer's methodologies about using smart, cost-effective ways to increase profits and build their businesses for the long haul. Many of you may have already invested in his BGS Marketing System and are using it with great results.

But no matter how you may have learned about him, Bill Glazer has emerged on the retail scene as more than just a "talking head..." Certainly he's not your cheesy motivational speaker type. Still, his "bootcamp-style" presentations have left attendees energized and geared up to employ Glazer's "outside-the-box" marketing strategies.

According to Dan S. Kennedy, the nation's leading marketing "guru," Bill Glazer is the #1 most celebrated marketing advisor to the retail industry, with hundreds of top stores nationwide utilizing his innovative direct-response advertising and direct mail ideas, lab tested with his own two exceptionally successful Baltimore stores.

A DAVID AGAINST GOLIATH

Today's independent retailers often feel like they are in the fight of their lives, up against juggernauts ranging from Wal-Mart, the biggest behemoth of all, to superstores in each specialty category, like Home Depot and Lowes in hard-

ware, Best Buy in electronics, Barnes & Noble in books, and so on.

In downtown Baltimore, there once were fourteen competing Menswear stores, each independently and locally owned – just like in many cities. Over a handful of years, as suburban malls proliferated and giant national chain stores entered the market, thirteen of those stores - some there for decades – closed their doors. The last store standing, Gage "World Class" Menswear, captained by Bill Glazer, has not only survived, it has prospered beyond any rational expectation. In fact, in recent years, while the entire menswear retailing industry has been in the doldrums, and independent stores everywhere have struggled just to stay even, Bill's downtown store, as well as his suburban location, have enjoyed double-digit annual growth and per square foot profits roughly 250% better than the industry average.

How can this be? What is Bill's secret?

The answer: Bill's strategies for prospering against all odds have made him something of a celebrity in his industry, and propelled him into a second business as a top marketing and business consultant to over 700 retail store owners nationwide in over 37 different categories.

FORGET ALL ABOUT
"NORMAL" RETAIL ADVERTISING

Bill probably spends less on advertising than most other stores his size because he does such a phenomenal job of maximizing value from his

306

own mailing list, which now tops 57,000. But even farther outside the norms of marketing in retail are the ways he supports his ads and mailings with technology-based automatic marketing. For example, Bill frequently uses voice-broadcast blasts to call all his customers and leave messages on their answering machines or voice mail instantaneously. "For less than ten cents a call, I deliver a message in my own voice to thousands of my customers within minutes," Bill explains. "This has increased response to a mailing by as much as 92%."

DRAGGING AN "OLD" INDUSTRY INTO 21ST CENTURY DIRECT MARKETING

"The retail business is still largely comprised of second, third, and even fourth generation family businesses, both blessed and cursed with traditions," Bill says, "now up against the equivalent of Wal-Mart in big chains and discounters. Independent stores cannot compete on price, yet are woefully behind the times in use of smart marketing strategies, technology, and alternative media. The salvation and prosperity of my own stores have been entirely due to my literally turning my back on the way retail stores have always advertised and operated, going outside the industry, and returning with direct marketing completely foreign to our business, but proven elsewhere."

In less that three years, over 700 store owners have purchased Bill's Marketing System, began using his ads and mailings, started using technology he's introduced to them like voice broadcast and e-mail marketing, and are achieving truly remarkable results. For example, a Texas owner says he completely revamped his mailings due to Bill, and with one promotion did 6 months worth of business in just 2 weeks! A Nebraska store owner with 25 years' experience hesitantly tried one of Bill's ideas and had a record-breaking week of sales. There are hundreds of such success stories in Bill's files and on display *(with full store names and locations)* at his website: www.billglazermarketing.com

In 2000, the industry journal MR Magazine named Bill and his BGS Marketing System to the list of the 100 Top People, Places, and Things Impacting the Industry at the Millennium…the equivalent of being named to People or Time Magazine's list of 100 most noteworthy or influential individuals. Bill also writes a monthly column on marketing for MR and several other retail newsletters.

Maybe even more important than any specific promotion is the way Bill guides his clients to an entirely new and different way of thinking about their businesses. Randy Diamond, owner of 22 retail stores, some of the oldest throughout northeastern Ohio, says: "I was brought up in the old school, that if you bought well, merchandised well, and had a good staff on the floor, business would increase. But we

found it difficult to get additional growth in recent years. Bill's focus on continuous, proactive marketing is key. This was a reorientation of my mind-set. The results have been phenomenal."

"Retailers in all categories have been conditioned to focus on merchandising, staffing, and newspaper or radio advertising. While all of these things are important, they are no longer enough," Bill explains. "We place more emphasis on marketing to our own list of past and present customers than on mass advertising. Being in the business of marketing your stores vs. operating your stores really is a distinctly different way of thinking."

In his position as these retailers' guide to the brave new world, Bill says he must coach them on new ways of thinking about their role in their business, their relationship with their customers, their competitive positioning, as well as the nuts-and-bolts of more effective advertising and profitable direct-mail. Perhaps the shining jewel of Bill's accomplishments was his winning the prestigious RAC Award at the 2002 Retail Advertising Conference. This honor is equivalent in retail as the Oscars are to movies and the Emmys to television. Imagine an independent retailer competing and winning against giants like Target, Wal-Mart, Chevrolet, Best Buy and Payless Shoe Source.

> "The top 5% of retailers don't see themselves as retailers, but as marketers of a retail business."
>
> *-- Bill Glazer*

BILL GLAZER TAKES ON THE ENTIRE SPECTRUM OF RETAIL

It seems that the independent and small-chain retailers in all product categories share common challenges, including their David vs. Goliath battles with "big box" superstores and discounters, increasing advertising clutter, and public resistance to traditional advertising. It turns out that the solutions Bill has pioneered, first with his own stores, are readily transferred to all types of retail.

Bill's first testing beyond his own industry was with retail stores selling outdoor equipment, camping goods, and sporting goods – and the first campaign he created for them generated an amazing 7-million dollars in sales for just $200,000.00 in marketing costs, in just 60 days. For an auto dealership, one of Bill's sales letters and a voice-broadcast campaign created over $250,000.00 in sales, from a total expenditure of $557.00.

Others enthusiastically embracing his system include owners of hardware stores, home and garden centers, gift shops, furniture stores, bicycle shops, womenswear, children's stores, formalwear, private postal centers, etc, etc.

In 2000, the U.S. Small Business Administration selected Bill Glazer as one of the top two business-people of the year for the state of Maryland.

GLAZER TEACHES RETAILERS AT "MAGIC" IN LAS VEGAS

Recently at MAGIC in Las Vegas, Bill presented to 240-plus mens' and womens' clothing retailers a menu of today's key marketing pitfalls and the appropriate business-building strategies to help avoid them. The following pages of seminar abstracts will come as a great service to those who weren't fortunate enough to attend, and are still scratching their heads trying to figure out how to turn the profit wheel in their favor.

"Lousy Ads Get Lousy Results," said Glazer at his presentation. He went on further to explain: "One of the services that I offer the members of my Marketing System is FREE critiques of their ads and direct mail pieces. As you can imagine, with over 700 members, I see a lot of ads every year. Here is what I have discovered - LOUSY ADS GET LOUSY RESULTS.

This is particularly instructive, because often-times retailers tell me that a particular media doesn't work. It might be postcards, sales letters, newspaper ads, radio or TV spots - whatever. When in reality, they all work. Some work better than others, and clearly my personal favorite is some form of direct mail. But retailers that run lousy ads and get lousy results mistakenly blame the media, when in actuality, it's the fault of the lousy ads."

The 10 Biggest Advertising Mistakes Made by Retailers

Let me tell you the "Ten Biggest Advertising Mistakes That Retailers Make" and the impact that they can have on the effectiveness of your advertising.

#1: Far and away, the biggest advertising mistake is having a Lousy Headline: When I write an ad or direct mail piece for a client, or for myself, I normally spend half of my time developing the headline. In fact, typically I will write about a dozen headlines before I settle on the one that I think will get the best response. The headline is the most important part of any ad. It will grab the readers' attention and pull them into what you have to say. Headlines like...

"Biggest Sale Ever"

"End Of Season Clearance"

"We're The #1 Men's Store in Hastings, Nebraska"

...are typically worthless.

What you really want to write is a headline that offers a benefit and provokes curiosity. For example, instead of writing a headline that reads, " Super Sale" try "Discover The (name of store) Super Sale That Other (category type) Stores Don't Want You To Know About!" Now, which one creates more curiosity? Which will get the prospect to read the rest of the ad?

> ## "Lousy ads get lousy results."
>
> *-- Bill Glazer*

#2: No Offer/Lousy Offer: It is very difficult and often costly to get a new customer in your store. What will make someone respond? Well, I'll tell you one thing - there is no way that someone will respond to a lousy offer, or worse yet, no offer. Remember, the real money in getting a new customer is in making them a "customer for life." That way, you'll reap your dividends when they return over and over again.

#3: No Deadline Or "Wimpy" Deadline: People are natural procrastinators. Unless you motivate them to respond NOW, they never do. A deadline is what makes them respond. Deadlines create fear - fear of losing out on a particular offer or opportunity. One rule that I live by is never to give a prospect more than a 2-week deadline. If you do, you might as well save your hard earned money that you invested in the ad.

#4: Lack Of Testimonials: What your current customers say about you is ten to twenty times more believable than what you say about yourself. Testimonials are a great way to get instant credibility with prospects. How many testimonials should you use? As many as you can - and use them everywhere.

#5: Lack Of A Guarantee Or A "Wimpy" Guarantee: This is a very simple concept but often scares retailers to death. Retail study after retail study has proven that the better the guarantee, the more people will buy. Sure, some will take advantage of your guarantee, but they are insignificant to the number that will buy more. Oh, by the way, if you can't guarantee your products or services, then find something else to sell.

#6: Me-Too Appearance: I have written and developed hundreds of ads and direct mail pieces during my career. Far and away, the most successful one that I have ever sent my customers was a 5-page, handwritten letter on yellow legal paper. Why was this so successful? Because it didn't look like an ad. Or in other words it didn't have a "me-too" appearance. Instead, it looked nothing like a traditional ad, but like a letter that a friend would send to a friend, resulting in my stores being filled with customers for two straight weeks.

#7: Focus On The Business Instead Of WIIFM: How many times do you see an ad for a particular business and all it says is how wonderful the business is? It talks about how many years they have been in business, or the friendly service, or the big selection. But, what about what the customer really wants? Customers ONLY want one thing – WIIFM (What's In It For Me).

#8: Trying To Accomplish Multiple Objectives: This is one of my personal pet peeves that I often see in bad advertising. The store or ad agency that created the ad often tries to accomplish multiple objectives. An ad should ONLY have one objective. All you

should care about is GETTING A STORE VISIT. A store visit is the only thing that can put money in your bank account. Image can't do that. Last time I tried, the teller at my local bank wouldn't allow me to deposit "image."

#9: Failure To Tell Your Story: Customers and prospects like a story. They want to hear why you are making the offer that you are making. It seems to add credibility, and when they believe you, they respond better. Plus, tell everything about your business that you can and don't take anything for granted. Things such as brands you carry, sizes, departments, methods of payment you accept, street address, phone number, etc., etc. should never be left out. The inclusion of any one of the above items on the list might be just the thing that makes the prospect respond.

#10: Cute: Why is so much advertising "cute?" Two reasons. First of all, cute advertising is the type that wins awards, and ad agencies like to win awards in order to help them "pitch" new clients. Also, advertisers like cute advertising because they think it gets remembered. Well, let me ask you a question? Can you give me the names of the advertisers that spent over a million dollars each during the last Super Bowl in order to air their 30-second TV commercial? Bet you can't name more than one or two. That's because cute advertising is remembered for being cute, but not for selling anything. Study after study has proven that the type of advertising that sells is still emotional, direct response advertising and not the "cute" brand-building type.

10 Leading Advertising "MEGA Mistakes" Most Often Made by Retailers:

1) Lousy Headline
2) No Offer or a Lousy Offer
3) No Deadline or a "Wimpy" Deadline
4) Lack of Testimonials
5) Lack of Guarantee or a "Wimpy" Guarantee
6) "Me-Too" Appearance
7) Focus on "WIIFM" Instead of Your Business
8) Trying to Accomplish Multiple Objectives
9) Failure to Tell Your Story
10) Cute

BILL GLAZER'S 3-STEP BUSINESS-BUILDING FORMULA

By way of introduction, let me give you some insights into just how powerful this is. In my 28-years of being a retailer, attending dozens and dozens of marketing conferences, buying every book and tape on marketing I could get my hands on, personally being mentored by the top marketing minds in the country, and working with over 1000 clients or members of my Marketing System, I have discovered that The 3-Step Business-Building System is the ONLY System that any company can use to grow their business. There are no other choices.

Now you can fight this if you want, but I'm telling you that this is powerful. Not because what I am about to share with you is so new. Actually, to most of you this will be common sense. But the power is in knowing the "3 Steps" and more importantly, how to use them to your benefit.

The first step of the "Business-Building Formula" is **Acquiring More New Customers**. In fact, typically

whenever I speak to retailers, this is what they always tell me-- "Everything would be okay if I could just get more new customers."

Now, that's pretty profound, isn't it? Everything would be okay if I just got new customers. The truth is, getting a new customer is not an easy task and can often be a rather expensive one, although it doesn't necessarily have to be.

For example, in my Marketing System that I provide to retailers, I teach 11 different strategies to "cost effectively" attract new customers. Let me show you one that is very cost efficient and works like a charm.

Question? Do you know what percentage of gift certificates never get redeemed? Well the national average is 18% and I'm willing to bet that yours is right around that number. So, have you ever thought about the unthinkable? How about discounting the purchase of gift certificates right around Christmas?

Here's why this strategy is so important to consider. 18% never get redeemed. So, if you give a discount of approximately 18% on the purchase of your gift certificates, you're actually breaking even with the non-redemption. But here's the real kicker. Do you know that 47% of all customers that redeem gift certificates actually spend twice the face value and a whopping 89% will spend more? Conversely, that sweater that they are buying from your store to give as a gift results in no additional purchase unless you are lucky enough for them to bring it back for an exchange.

And one more benefit...most of the gift certificates that are purchased for Christmas gifts get redeemed in January; just when you are looking for customers.

Now this happens to be a very good new customer acquisition strategy. But the important thing to really learn here is what is the true objective of acquiring new customers. The real objective should be to get them into your database so you can continue to market to them in the future. Because that's the real value of a customer. It's been coined – CUSTOMERS FOR LIFE.

So, now we have these customers in our database. We are ready to move on the second step of our Three-Step-Business-Building-System, which is **Getting the Customers We Have to Return - MORE OFTEN**. Otherwise, you will go broke if you simply rely on constantly attracting new customers.

But before I show you a promotion designed to accomplish this, let's take just a minute to look at **"Why Customers Do Not Come Back."** When customers are surveyed, far and away the number one reason why they do NOT return is that "they *forget." (You might be surprised to hear that price is number five.) Now what does this tell you? You have to constantly remind them to come back. The strategy that I'm going to show you is a campaign that many members of my Marketing System have copied practically AS-IS. It is designed to bring in a steady stream of past customers to your store for six consecutive weeks.*

Here's how it works...

On **day 1** *a postcard is mailed. Then on* **day 15** *a second postcard is mailed to the same list. Next, on* **day 29** *a third postcard is mailed. Finally on* **day 36** *a voice broadcast message is left on your customers' answering machines.*

Now, here are the results: (see chart to the immediate right)

So here's the BIG LESSON that you should have learned: If I stopped at just one postcard like most do, look at all the additional business I would have left on the table. In this case, an additional two-thirds. This multi-step sequence of marketing is critically important.

Results from the 3-Step "You Decide What's on Sale" Business-Building Campaign:

	Quantity	Response	%	$$ Generated
Postcard #1	9,513	181	1.9%	$49,190.77
Postcard #2	9,227	151	1.6%	$35,837.26
Postcard #3	9,134	236	2.6%	$75,545.28
Voice Broadcast	4,750			
Total		568	6.1%	$160,573.31

Outcome: 13 to 1 Return On Investment!

Now we come to the last step, which is the most profitable step there is, and ironically is the one that most retailers seem to totally or at least partially ignore. This step is **Getting the Customers You Already Have in Your Store to Spend More During Each Visit.**

Obviously, this is the most profitable step because it involves no expensive marketing costs at all. Customers are already in the store, so you do NOT have to spend any money on advertising to get them there. They are right where you want them. But what are you doing to encourage them to spend more? Just think a minute at what would happen to your business if each customer spent fifty dollars more every time they shop in your stores. Just multiply every transaction by fifty dollars. That would be a sizeable amount of money and cure a lot of your problems.

You can see why this is my favorite of the 3-Step Business-Building System and why it is so important to realize all three steps, especially this one.

I'll show you one of the seven different strategies I teach in order to get your customers to spend more during each visit. This strategy is called a "Frequent Buyer Program" and every store should have one.

Roughly, here's how the program works: For every $50 that the customer spends, he or she receives a

stamp on the card. When the card is complete, the customer receives an additional $50 of FREE merchandise. Now, you might need to modify this for your particular store.

What is important about this program and why every store should have one is the fact that it accomplishes two steps out of the 3-Step Business-Building Formula.

Obviously, it encourages your customers to return to your stores more often. In fact, the first 3 years that we had this program in place, we actually tracked it and found that our customers returned on average one additional trip a year. You can imagine that this translates into a big number.

But what is perhaps more important is what this program does while the customer is in the store. For instance, a savvy salesperson can use this as an incentive to get his customers to buy that "big ticket item" in order to receive the additional $50 savings. I can tell you first hand that this little card has been responsible for us selling a lot of customers a second suit while they are in one of my stores.

Then there is the more practical application: The customer gets to the counter with $239.00 worth of merchandise and you tell them to pick out $11 more of socks or underwear to get up to the next box. Multiply these $11 additional purchases by a lot of people. I think you can see the magic in a program like this.

Bottom line: *Customers absolutely love these programs and retailers reap greater sales!* END

- CD of an **EXCLUSIVE GOLD AUDIO INTERVIEW:**

  These are EXCLUSIVE interviews with <u>successful users of direct response advertising, leading experts and entrepreneurs in direct marketing, and famous business authors and speakers</u>. Use them to turn commuting hours into "POWER Thinking" hours.

* The New Member No B.S.® Income Explosion Guide & CD (Value = $29.97)

This resource is <u>especially designed for NEW MEMBERS</u> to show them HOW they can join the thousands of Established Members **creating exciting sales and PROFIT growth** in their Business, Practices, or Sales Careers & Greater SUCCESS in their Business lives.

Income Explosion FAST START Tele-Seminar with Dan Kennedy, Bill Glazer, and Lee Milteer (Value = $97.00)

Attend from the privacy and comfort of your home or office...hear a DYNAMIC discussion <u>of Key Advertising, Marketing, Promotion, Entrepreneurial & Phenomenon strategies</u>, PLUS answers to the most Frequently Asked Questions about these Strategies

* You'll also get these Exclusive "Members Only" Perks:

- **Special FREE Gold Member CALL-IN TIMES:** Several times a year, Dan & I schedule Gold-Member ONLY Call-In times
- **Gold Member RESTRICTED ACCESS WEBSITE**: Past issues of the *No B.S.® Marketing Letter*, articles, special news, etc.
- **Continually Updated MILLION DOLLAR RESOURCE DIRECTORY** with Contacts and Resources Dan & his clients use.

To activate your MOST INCREDIBLE FREE GIFT EVER you only pay a one-time charge of $4.95 (or $8.95 for Int'l subscribers) to cover postage (this is for everything). **After your 1-Month FREE test-drive, you will automatically continue at the <u>lowest</u> Gold Member price of $59.97 per month. Should you decide to cancel your membership, you can do so at any time by calling Glazer-Kennedy Insider's Circle™ at 410-825-8600 or faxing a cancellation note to 410-825-3301 (Monday through Friday 9am – 5pm). Remember, your credit card will NOT be charged the low monthly membership fee until the beginning of the next month, which means you will receive 1 full issue to read, test, and** profit from all of the powerful techniques and strategies you get from being an Insider's Circle Gold Member. **And of course, it's impossible for you to lose, because if you don't absolutely LOVE everything you get, you can simply cancel your membership before next month and never get billed a single penny for membership.**

EMAIL REQUIRED IN ORDER TO NOTIFY YOU ABOUT THE GLAZER-KENNEDY UNIVERSITY WEBINARS AND FAST START TELESEMINAR

Name _____ Business Name _____

Address _____

City _____ State _____ Postal Code _____ Country _____

e-mail* _____

Phone _____ Fax_____

Credit Card Instructions to Cover $4.95 ($8.95 Int'l) for Shipping & Handling:

_____Visa _____MasterCard _____ American Express _____ Discover

Credit Card Number _____ Exp. Date _____

Signature _____ Date _____

FAX BACK TO 410-825-3301
Or mail to: 401 Jefferson Ave, Towson, MD 21286